A holiday club for all the family

Messy Church® is a registered word mark and the logo is a registered device mark of
The Bible Reading Fellowship

Text copyright © Lucy Moore 2015
Illustrations copyright © Simon Smith 2015

The author asserts the moral right
to be identified as the author of this work

Published by
The Bible Reading Fellowship
15 The Chambers, Vineyard
Abingdon OX14 3FE
United Kingdom
Tel: +44 (0)1865 319700
Email: enquiries@brf.org.uk
Website: www.brf.org.uk
BRF is a Registered Charity

ISBN 978 0 85746 305 0

First published 2015
10 9 8 7 6 5 4 3 2 1 0

Acknowledgements
Unless otherwise stated, scripture quotations are taken from the Contemporary English Version of the Bible published by HarperCollins Publishers, copyright © 1991, 1992, 1995 American Bible Society.

pp. 29–30: 'The sower' is reproduced from *The Gospels Unplugged* by Lucy Moore (Barnabas for Children, 2002). Used with permission.

Cover photos: Cover photos: Parachute game and girl in spotty dress © Ben Mizen; Blue twirly ribbon © Tomjac80/iStock/Thinkstock; Pencils © Krzysztof Nieciecki/iStock/Thinkstock; Paint © Olga Danylenko/iStock/Thinkstock; Balloons © nikkytok/iStock/Thinkstock; Background © MAHESH PURANIK/iStock/Thinkstock.

Every effort has been made to trace and contact copyright owners for material used in this resource. We apologise for any inadvertent omissions or errors, and would ask those concerned to contact us so that full acknowledgement can be made in the future.

A catalogue record for this book is available from the British Library

Printed by Gutenberg Press, Tarxien, Malta

A holiday club for all the family

Lucy Moore

Thanks to...

William Groves, whose generosity got the ball rolling

David Brindley, Rosemary Fairfax and the team at Portsmouth Cathedral

Alex Hughes, Rona Stuart-Bourne, Alex Lihou and the team at St Peter's

Martyn Payne, whose creative energy knows no bounds

those who have shared their stories

and all of you who give so generously of your time and talents
to make other Messy Family Fun Clubs happen

Contents

This should be going on in more churches, to **involve families**.
DAWN LEANING

It's an amazing thing for children. My kids always have fun in a **safe and friendly environment**.
JODIE JOSEPH

It was great to **bring people from the community together**.
THE HAMMERTON FAMILY

Very entertaining, lots to do, **good fun**.
TRACEY HAMMERTON

Nice to come and relax, have a cup of tea. Food for the children, time to socialise. **Something for every age**.
LIZ DARBYSHIRE

If one of the values of a 'mission-shaped church' is that it should be related to its context, then the Messy Family Fun Club has added huge value to our church life. **Nothing else we've tried has had anything like the same impact**.
REVD DR ALEX HUGHES

How our first Messy Family Fun Club came about

This starts off as a very Anglican story, but I hope you'll see how the end result can be used in any setting, just as Messy Church itself is used by all the main Christian denominations.

A generous man called William Groves died and left an unexpectedly large legacy to Portsmouth Cathedral. The Cathedral Chapter (the cathedral's governing body) felt that it would be right to spend the money on more than drainpipes and roof tiles, essential though those are. They asked the Dean (in charge of the day-to-day running of the cathedral), David Brindley, to use some of it to further outreach to children and young people.

The Dean asked me, as a Lay Canon of the cathedral—duties unclear to me except that I got to wear a very posh Hogwarts-esque robe on occasion and could presumably have been fired (canon, get it? Never mind…) by the bishop if the worst came to the worst—to suggest how we might use the money to fund some sort of Messy outreach work to families and young people. He also wondered if it would be possible to work not just in the cathedral but in one of the churches in Portsmouth city centre (St Peter's)

that lacked the financial resources to make something like this happen on its own. Could we run a holiday club for families along the lines of Messy Church, but every day for a week rather than once a month?

Could we indeed? The Dean and the staff of St Peter's chatted and got excited. I stuck a pencil in my ear and pondered. The BRF team added their wisdom, ideas and encouragement and, after many meetings and much planning, some heartache but surprisingly little pain (at least, no one told me about any), our first Messy Family Fun Club ran in the Easter holiday of 2013.

This resource is the product of that event and draws together the experiences and wisdom of the generous people who gave up their time and skills to get messy with us. Of course, we were by no means the first church to run an all-age holiday club, and I'm very grateful to those who have contributed their own stories, materials and plans to add value to your own ministry. We'll collect more suggestions on the website and on the 'Messy Church Mag' Facebook page as time goes by and the ideas are refined.

*

Why run an all-age holiday club?

Why didn't we simply advertise a traditional five-day event for children and draw on the huge amount of high-quality material already available?

Well, one of the reasons why Messy Church started in the first place, in 2004, was our observation that the families of the children who go to a church's holiday club rarely want any more connection with the church apart from free childminding for that week. So the good seed that has been sown in helping children make a step towards Jesus falls all too often into the rocky part of the field (to use Jesus' parable in Luke 8), as children return home and receive no encouragement to pursue their journey. The parent or carer has not taken part in the experience and cannot provide help as a fellow traveller on the journey, and the family's values may be a million miles away from the values that the children have been exploring at the holiday club.

But... if the whole family could come on a journey together towards Jesus—if they could all see the love of God in action in their local church and share the same experience of lives being transformed—surely there would be more chance of the seed taking root?

Portsmouth Cathedral was giving us the chance to take Messy Church back to its moment of germination and devise a holiday club package that would bring parents, carers, grandparents and other significant adults together with their children to go on a life-changing journey. It was time to reinvent.

As I've said, we were by no means the first Messy Church team to run a holiday club with the values of Messy Church. The website (**www.messychurch.org.uk**) had gathered news of several happening in different parts of the country, but nothing I had read about so far was quite what we were trying to do. One Messy Church holiday club had developed from a very successful long-running Churches Together children-only holiday club. In order to remain in line with what families had been expecting each summer, the team sensibly decided to invite younger children to come accompanied by an adult, and older children to come on their own. Their programme ran Messy Church with the family groups while the un-accompanied children were given a choice of sport, art, drama or dance workshops; everyone then came together at the end of the week. However, we didn't need to take into account any expectations based on an established approach. We had a clean slate, so we decided that, just as in Messy Church itself, all children would need to be accompanied unless they were helping on the team.

Running Messy Church on consecutive days presented certain challenges. We realised that there would be a different dynamic when the sessions were so close to each other. A daily Messy Family Fun Club would feel more like a holiday club than the monthly Messy Church: it wouldn't be tied to school finishing times, nobody would be in uniform, no one would be in a hurry to arrive or to leave and there'd be a little more pressure to keep the energy up. Could we find a way to hold on to the values and main elements while making the most of the more focused community to add something different—something that would also serve to maintain a high level of energy, engagement and commitment?

Advantages of the Messy Family Fun Club

A Messy Family Fun Club is great fun for families and for the team. It's an opportunity to make friendships, to explore the story of Jesus and to encounter him in the Bible-based activities, in the love of God's people, in the stranger, in prayer and worship and around meal tables. These are all healthy signs of the kingdom of God. It's an opportunity for the church to welcome members of the wider community and help them to have ownership of their local church. It's a chance for families to enjoy learning new skills, expressing their creativity in a safe space, getting a satisfying meal and experiencing first-hand what a church community can be like.

This is true of a normal Messy Church, but a Messy Family Fun Club may well work on a more intense level and speed up the pace and progress of all these developments. It also offers freedom to build more closely on the ideas of the previous days, as people are more likely to remember them than if they were presented a month ago. Learning songs and prayers is likewise much easier. A Messy Family Fun Club is a chance to provide holiday activities for the families in your neighbourhood who don't have the resources to get away for a break, and food for those who are living on the edge of poverty.

Additionally:

- It's an opportunity for families who can't make it to a normal Messy Church to join in the church community (for example, if the children are usually away at school or parents are working).
- There's more chance that the day's activities and learning will be talked, sung or prayed about at home if the adults have taken part in it too.
- The ratio of leaders to families is not as stringent as it is for a children-only club.
- Leaders are responsible only for their part in the programme, not for looking after the children.
- It's an opportunity to develop a more demanding piece of artwork throughout the week, with elements being added each day. For example, you might consider making a banner, flags or a sculpture, using papier mâché, modelling with Modroc, or making paper, crystal gardens, a proper prayer tree or 'stained-glass' windows—all those fun activities that can never be finished in time at a normal Messy Church.
- There's scope to do slightly more 'risky' activities, as parents/carers can always keep their children away from them if they wish.
- First aiders will be less busy than at an ordinary holiday club, as a parent is more likely than a leader to say, 'Pull yourself together! It's only a bump! I'll kiss it better!' and other bracing and medicinal words that reduce the need for an incident to be recorded in the Accident Book.
- Adults need to play in order to be balanced human beings. Why should children have all the fun?

Disadvantages of the Messy Family Fun Club

Essentially, most of the pros and cons that apply to Messy Church, with its all-age format, apply to the Messy Family Fun Club too.

- Some families won't be able to come, as parents will be working or the whole family will be away on holiday.
- It runs the risk of attracting only very young families.
- It doesn't provide childcare.
- Putting on a range of activities that includes adults is more difficult than finding activities for children only.
- All-age celebrations are more challenging than children-only ones.

- Some adults try to dissociate themselves from the activities and celebration, becoming an emotional drain on the community.
- Some leaders feel shy about introducing an activity to adults and are worried about being criticised.
- Some leaders try to treat the club as an educational experience rather than an opportunity for worship and fun. This attitude can express itself in directive leading that makes adults feel infantilised.

If you already run a Messy Church

The Messy Family Fun Club is a wonderful way to fast-track friendships that are inevitably built slowly at a once-a-month gathering. You might finally disentangle which brother is Josh and which is Dan, or remember the difference between the cousins Tia and Lucia, if you see them every day for a week! It will also encourage the families to feel more ownership of the monthly Messy Church. I can imagine people volunteering to join the team or suggesting their own ideas more readily if they are having daily contact with the team for five days.

A Messy Family Fun Club is an opportunity to:

- intentionally pray for and work with families who you sense may be wanting something more than the monthly Messy Church can offer.
- invite your regular families to help lead an activity as a one-off, to take the first steps in joining the team.
- build on any gifts and talents you've observed in the families or team, such as drama, music or dance, and plan activities round these talents.
- learn new songs and prayers.
- have one table each day dedicated to an overt faith development opportunity (such as Table Talk, Quiz the Vicar, Auntie Pat's Problem Corner or Extreme Craft) and see if any have the potential to be continued at Messy Church itself.

If you don't already run a Messy Church

If, like Portsmouth Cathedral and St Peter's, you haven't yet started a Messy Church, a holiday club is a great way of showcasing what it's going to feel like and to start the Messy Church with a sense of community, from working with families you already know.

A Messy Family Fun Club is an opportunity to:

- get to know people relatively quickly and earn goodwill and trust.
- create a community with the values, boundaries and behaviours you need to develop in your future Messy Church.
- listen to what families need from the church.
- gauge what the families and team have to offer by way of skills, resources and equipment.
- make a monthly Messy Church seem ridiculously easy by comparison!

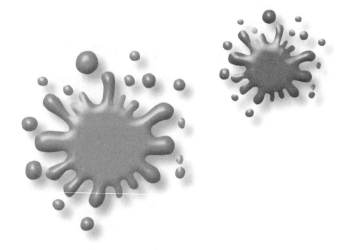

*

Suggestions for follow-up

You need to create a reason for families to stay in touch and come back. You want to keep on remembering the names of those you've got to know. You want to continue building friendships and be there for people over a period of time. Some of these ideas may be helpful and feasible:

- Have a prayer activity available in church that recalls the names or faces of the families who came to the Messy Family Fun Club. Encourage the other congregations to pray for them, or simply bring the families into the prayers of the church during the services.
- During the Messy Family Fun Club, shoot a DVD (or, better, get the teenagers to do it) of what happens and invite the families to a film night soon afterwards.
- As part of the feedback, make sure you ask what the families would like the church to provide next and whether they would consider being part of the team that would make it happen.
- At the Messy Family Fun Club itself, get as many families as are willing to 'like' a Facebook page, which can then be used to put up photos, keep people informed of other events and make it easy for them to communicate with you.
- Put a related event in the diary a month after the Messy Family Fun Club and for the following two months: a Messy Church session is the most straightforward, but it could be a social, a meal or an outing.
- Take CDs or prints of Messy Family Fun Club photos round to people's houses soon after the Messy Family Fun Club and use the opportunity to continue your relationship. Ask if there's anything they want from the church and give them a reminder of any future events.
- If a particular activity goes down really well at the Messy Family Fun Club, look for imaginative ways to expand it into a further event or ministry. For example, if sewing was popular, plan a sewing afternoon to build on skills. If exploding cola bottles was the key moment, plan an event based on wild science. If the cookery went down well, have a family cake bake. The main aim is to develop friendships around the activities; church can develop around the friendships in due course.
- If any of the families are having a baptism (or, indeed, a wedding or funeral) during usual service times, encourage them to invite other families to the service too.
- Write up press releases reporting on the Messy Family Fun Club and send them with photos to your local newspapers.

*

Team roles

Most of the team members will hold down several of the roles below. Plan on trying to find 20 to 30 people who will commit to the week or to one or more days. This will give you room to accommodate the inevitable drop-out. Your volunteers may be whole families, children or teens doing their International Baccalaureat Community Service or their Duke of Edinburgh Award. Team members may be in their 90s; they may be members of your Messy Church or friends of friends. Book them in plenty of time to get their DBS checks done if required and to give them time to get used to the idea of what you're attempting. If they're under 18, make sure a permission form is completed and held on file.

See appendices

Young helpers form (page 68)
Risk assessment form (page 72)
Safeguarding policy (page 74)

- **The planning team:** four or five competent people who are passionate about making the Messy Family Fun Club work. Include a minister of the church and your Alan (see below).
- **The 'Alan':** a crucial role. This is the person who worries about everything, administers it all and has no other job than to troubleshoot, get the numbers right, make sure lunch is organised on time, ensure access to the tap (even if the formidable Lunch Club is in progress), find new loo rolls, rush out to buy milk, check the PA is working, get the mic back from the power-mad teenager who has run off with it and so on, *and is still smiling by the end of the day.* Named after the inimitable Alan Lihou. Every church needs one.

- **The team leader:** carries the can. The buck stops here. This person delegates or does what needs doing, checks and doublechecks all the leaders for all the jobs, runs the meetings, makes the final decisions about what happens, coordinates and prays a lot.
- **The publicity person:** someone who will design good publicity to make sure everyone knows about the Messy Family Fun Club.
- **The administrator:** someone to take bookings before the event and be at the end of a phone for enquiries (for example, to tell people that they can't just drop their children off).
- **The back-up prayer team:** regular congregation members who commit to praying before and during the event.
- **The follow-up person:** responsible for everything that will give the week longevity and lasting impact.
- **The welcome team:** two or three people who are on the door to welcome and register people. (The rest of the team can be 'floating' welcomers.)
- **The barista:** serves drinks throughout the morning. May be a small team or just one person.
- **The opening games leader:** runs ten minutes of filler games every day. The rest of the team joins in.
- **The MC:** the person who runs the opening gathering and the celebration.
- **The musicians and/or technicians**
- **The 'dancers':** to lead action songs.
- **The storyteller:** can be the same person as the MC.
- **The pray-er:** can be the same person as the MC.
- **The activity leaders:** ten to 20 people.
- **The extreme skills leaders:** three to five people per day.
- **The cooks:** four to six people.
- **The clear-up team**

*

Programme and timings

Here are the details of what we did. Don't follow this outline slavishly but adapt and improve it for your own circumstances. We repeated this programme each day, starting at 3.00 pm (with dinner at 6.30 pm).

8.30–9.15 am	Team arrive and prepare
9.15 am	Team prayer and meeting
10.00 am	Welcome chill time with filler activity
10.10 am	Gathering
10.20 am	Fun activities with Bible theme
11.00 am	Coffee break/clear up crafts
11.10 am	Extreme family skills
11.45 am	Celebration
12.00	Lunch
1.00 pm	Clear up; set up if possible for next session; short team reflection

Team arrive and prepare (8.30–9.15 am)

Team members sign in as they arrive or are pursued by the Alan (see above). This is the time for the team members who are simply running an activity on the day to familiarise themselves with what they're running, how to do it and why they're doing it and to doublecheck that they have all the equipment and materials they need. Team members might want to carry a small bottle of hand sanitiser if there are any activities that involve food.

If you are the team leader, in your apron pocket/ haversack you may need tissues, hand wipes, a pen and notebook, a copy of who should be doing what and when at all times, a thick marker pen, a phone with team's numbers preloaded, keys to everywhere you need to access, emergency money for when the [milk/glue/chocolate buttons/face paint/you name it] runs out, and chocolate (optional—well, fairly optional).

Team prayer and meeting (9.15 am)

The team leader encourages the team to talk about what went well the day before (from Day 2 onward) and what could be improved today, then summarises the theme for the day. The team turns all this into prayer. Make time, too, for each leader to practise out loud what they will say to introduce their activity to the families who come to do it, if any of your team are remotely unsure of how to mention God without blushing. At this point, the Locks Heath team (see page 60) have their first cake input of the day, which is a sound idea.

Welcome chill time with filler activity (10.00 am)

The wonderful, warm welcome team are at the table by the door to make people feel at home and to register them. Handouts are given out, allergies are checked out, toilets are pointed out, coffee and juice are poured out and unaccompanied children are (gently) shown the way out.

As families start trickling or pouring in, they find their name badge or design a new name sticker for the day, and are then invited to join in a 'filler activity'. Parachute games worked well for us as they're visual, fun, inclusive and non-threatening; they create community, can absorb newcomers, are quick to set up and clear up and can easily stop at the drop of a hat.

Alternatively, large garden toys could be scattered around, such as giant Jenga, noughts and crosses, chess, badminton, pingpong, quoits, four-in-a-row, snakes and ladders, and jigsaws of varying degrees of difficulty.

One person needs to be in charge of this time, but the rest of the team need to be briefed to join in or be available to chat with families, rather than fussing over their activities. Hospitality is a joint effort. Think how you'd feel if you were coming into a strange place with your family.

There may also be ongoing projects that families can add to in any free moments, such as large-scale colouring activities, wall displays or big models from the day before.

Gathering (10.10 am)

This time is important for building up your community and making it clear to everyone what shape and theme the day will take. Don't be tempted to wait until more people arrive or you'll encourage a later start every day.

Gather the group together with a 'welcome' song. The same one every day helps people to learn it and to understand what it signals. Ask a leader to welcome everyone warmly, make all the running gags of the week that are bound to crop up and succinctly remind everyone of the rules. *(Adults, you're responsible for your children. Everyone, always make sure you know where your adult/child is. Don't leave the building without telling the leader. Walk, don't run.)* We thought we would need to include 'Mind your language', as some of the families might have standards of language that are different from what is appropriate in a church, but, to our great joy, we didn't hear a single swear word from start to finish. (And you know what these cathedral types are like!) The leader will also explain about toilets, fire escapes and fire procedures, introduce the day's theme and say a short prayer to bless people as they get started on the activities.

Fun activities with Bible theme (10.20 am)

This is like a standard Messy Church activities hour, with 40 minutes offering approximately ten activities, covering a range of approaches to explore the day's theme. Don't be tempted to skimp and have fewer activities. You need the variety, as you'll have people who learn and encounter God in many different ways and who have different needs. Remember, if you have 50 people coming, you don't need 50 sets of each activity; people will only have time to do a few, so 20 to 25 sets is usually enough unless you have hundreds of people.

Make sure each leader at each table is as well briefed as possible about what they're doing, how to do it, how to share the reason for doing the activity, how to leave as much to the people themselves to do as possible, any risk involved and how to handle that risk. We tried to allocate two leaders to each activity as this made it more fun and easier to have conversations with people. It also meant that we could pair someone who couldn't bend down with someone lithe and active, or someone experienced with someone less confident (although we didn't always have enough team members for this).

Encourage families to do as many or as few activities as they like, and expect them to take a day or so to find their feet and work out the boundaries and system. We definitely felt people relaxing and trusting more on the second and following days. For this slot, people flow from one activity to the next as they feel like it. Most of the activities are deliberately quite short.

Our saving grace was the purchase of ten large plastic tubs, into which we put all that was needed for each activity every day and which we then simply left at the table for the activity leader to unpack. Having the tubs meant that we could organise everything the night before rather than at the last minute. It also meant that everything on the table, rubbish and all, could simply be dumped in the tub at the end, so that the table could be used elsewhere.

As at a Messy Church, it's good to have a central supply of basic craft materials (paper, card, scissors, glue, pencils, paint, stickers, sticky tape and newspaper) and clean-up materials available to the team at any time. Cleaning fluids and creams should obviously be locked away, but cloths, wipes, kitchen roll and bin bags can all be readily accessible.

During this time, invite your barista to bring drinks to the team members who are marooned at their tables.

Please note: there are so many published Messy Church resources now that I'm sure I've used activities from some of them in this book. So that you don't feel cheated, I've tried to add alternatives and different versions as far as possible, but, to be honest, the families won't mind doing the same ones again if you've used them before and they worked the first time round. After all, which of us would not happily eat a pig biscuit every day of the week? And I'm sure you will have your own even more brilliant and varied ideas.

Coffee break (11.00 am)

For us, the coffee break turned out to be a very messy crossover between activities, but messy in a good way. It didn't feel disorganised or bossy; it was just a gradual, unfussed ending of one 'zone', then a short pause as we set up the next. We didn't have an organised 'sit down with a drink and now go to the toilet' time, as we might have had at a children-only club, but rather a continual flow of people being served drinks by our friendly barista throughout the activities beforehand. When the team was ready to roll, we gathered everyone together and described the options on offer in the next slot and where they were all running.

Some leaders worry about the proximity of hot drinks to lots of people, but in all the Messy Churches that have open-access hot drinks, I've never come across one that has found it dangerous. The presence of so many adults slows down movement and impedes rough behaviour.

Extreme family skills (11.10 am)

This is where we took the opportunity to do something a little different from our normal Messy Church activities. In this slot we invited people to choose one of three to five 'skills' and stick with it for the whole half hour rather than moving from one to another. This gave the leaders a chance to develop a skill or idea with a smaller group of people, without having to start explaining from scratch every two minutes. All the extreme skills were open to all ages, of course, although some activities appealed more to particular age groups, and some people meandered from one to another regardless, but that didn't matter in the bigger picture.

You can draw on the skills of your own team, wider church or local community for this part of the day. Our vision for this slot was to give families skills that would be useful practically in 'real life', not directly connected to a Bible story. We also wanted to offer people the opportunity to try out something they wouldn't otherwise have had the chance to try, and we wanted activities that celebrated our being part of the City of Portsmouth, helping people to take pride in their environment.

This slot turned out to be deeply rewarding and a time that we all appreciated, when we could spend longer concentrating on one thing and on one select group of people. 'Extreme' may be an exaggeration, but it is an intriguing and fun 'cover-all' title. One Messy Family Fun Club calls a similar section 'Classy Crafts', which is also a very good name—and last night I dreamed it was called 'Ultimate Crafts', which probably means I need to get out more.

We invited our diocesan experts to bring their skills, and although they couldn't all make it, our wonderful Diocesan Youth and Children's Adviser, Ben Mizen, came to run photography-on-your-mobile-phone workshops and also took professional-standard family portraits as souvenirs of the week. He has some interesting reflections on the spirituality of family photography as a result. The Fire Service generously came and let us pat their fire engine, set off the siren and flirt with the firemen, variously enjoyed by the different ages and genders. The delightful 14-year-old Daisy ran a dance workshop, completely unfazed when only tiny girls came with their mums. She swiftly turned her planned complex routines into something called simply 'Twirling with Daisy' and a marvellous time was had by all. Rona and her able assistants ran Family Cooking every day, with activities that either explored healthy eating or involved everybody in actually cooking a portion of a recipe they could also make at home—not easy, when the only facilities were microwaves and washing-up bowls, but very popular. The

amazing and unflappable Chris Cox and his team from Spirit in Sport (**www.spiritinsport.org.uk/about-us**) provided superb indoor sports in the nave (a big open space in the cathedral or down the centre of a church) every day, from hockey to football to games that saw boys and girls, mums and dads getting valuable exercise and having oodles of fun.

What else did we enjoy? Brass rubbing on the Mary Rose memorial, gardening, how to sew on a button (very well received), woodwork, drama and soap-carving a sheep. (Yes, yours truly once won the Lincolnshire Young Farmers' Prize for Soap Carving. Before you ask, I can only do sheep.) You're limited only by the skills of your extended church family and community. We ended up offering between three and five of the extreme skills each day, depending on the availability of people to lead them.

Alan Lihou from St Peter's writes:

When we first started to plan the Messy Family Fun Club, we endeavoured to get different organisations to attend during the week to demonstrate different extreme activities. However, due to various circumstances, this did not fully come to fruition.

We did, however, manage to get the Fire Service to bring a fire engine on one day. The children really loved climbing over the tender and into the cabin and looking at all the different types of fire-fighting equipment. We paid for a magician to attend one session to demonstrate some magic tricks, which was a real treat for many of the children and their families.

We then had to think about what skills the helpers had, which could be shown and taught to the families. A few of the helpers enjoyed cooking, so each day they showed a group some simple cooking-related task, which included icing a cake and making an egg-and-bacon bread pudding, which could be cooked in a microwave oven. The families really enjoyed learning these new skills and, of course, tasting the finished products; some of the dishes they made were really delicious.

One lady liked sewing, so the children were shown some simple tasks, such as sewing on buttons or making a simple pouch by sewing around a piece of material. The children were really proud of their finished items, which they were able to take home. Another lady showed a few children how to knit—another skill that the children loved to try. We purchased some reasonably priced plain white T-shirts and fabric pens, and the children could then decorate the garment to take home.

Other activities during the week included how to take a good photograph with a mobile telephone. We planted some seeds and plants in pots, which people could take home. We also taught some children a song and, on another occasion, gave a drama lesson.

What we found was that these relatively simple activities were very much enjoyed by all the children and their families. We learned that you do not need to have a really exciting extreme activity, which, at the planning stage, we were worried we would need, to keep the children's attention.

Celebration (11.45 am)

The celebration drew together the theme of the day and created a space for sung worship, prayer and communal listening to God's word. We kept it short, sang no more than two songs and had a story followed by a short prayer. We were blessed to have Alex the vicar on his guitar and Arthur the music student on his saxophone, with Daisy and Judith leading the actions and Martyn telling the stories and leading prayers, generally including the whole group in the experience with his enthusiasm and ability to open up awe and wonder amid the chaos. I seem to remember that my part in all this was a blur of taking photos, preventing a hyperactive Spiderman from killing himself by launching his small body optimistically from St Peter's pulpit, and watching people smiling, people frowning in concentration and people active in the actions of the songs, while I prayed for the friends and strangers there and wondered what was going on inside each one of them.

Please note: Bible story text is not provided in this book or as a website download because different teams will have different preferred versions, but it is easy to copy and paste the relevant passages from **www.biblegateway. com**.

Lunch (12.00)

The extreme skills used very few tables, so there was plenty of time to set up tables for the meal during the extreme skills slot, especially as the earlier activities had been 'tubbed'. We had the luxury of a larger-than-normal budget, so, to make life easier, we bought in platters of sandwiches and had a catering company provide hot meals on some of the days. (Favourite moment: an entire family meticulously removing all the fillings from their sandwiches and declaring happily, 'Lovely bread!') We also did a fish and chip run on the Friday. The plates and cups were disposable, raising green issues but eliminating the need for a washing-up team.

In these settings, where there was no dedicated catering team with a calling to hospitality, as many Messy Churches have or are developing, it made a lot of sense to buy in the food and use disposable equipment. But it made me realise how precious it is to have homemade food if at all possible: there is much more 'heart' involved and the day becomes much more of a personal community event than a professional production—more of a gift than a job. People are frankly more appreciative and grateful if they know the people who have been cooking for them.

The food itself becomes an offering and expression of love and friendship—not something I had thought about before.

Clear-up, set-up, short team reflection (1.00 pm)

This will inevitably be messy as families finish their meals at different rates and team members are dashing off to work and other commitments. As good hosts, set aside someone to say 'goodbye' at the door and remind people to take their works of art home. It is really helpful to have a completely separate 'clear-up team' who can come in bright-eyed and bushy-tailed and simply sort things out, ready for the next session. Spending a moment as a team checking that everyone is OK and saying 'thank you' to God and to each other is also a good investment.

Alan Lihou writes:

Although the Messy Family Fun Club was hard work, it was really enjoyable. It was wonderful that the members of the congregation of all ages could help and pass on their knowledge, by helping the families with the craft activities and the extreme skills, telling them and showing them the meaning of God's love.

It was lovely to see how proud the children were when they made anything they could take home to show the rest of their family, either from the craft activity or the new extreme skill they had learnt, which was as simple as sewing buttons in a design on a piece of cloth.

It is also amazing, because you are with the children for a week; they get to know you and you do not realise it. Three months after the Messy Family Fun Club, I attended a couple of local community events, and children and their parents spoke to me and said how much they had enjoyed the week and were looking forward to the next event, which I was able to tell them about. I have to be truthful: I did not remember them, but they certainly knew me.

*

FAQs

How many people will come?

Listen to my hollow laugh. See my shrugging shoulders. It depends on your existing connections with your community, the effort you put into publicity and, more than anything, the enthusiasm of your church members in 'gossiping' the prospect of the Messy Family Fun Club around the place.

Where and how do we publicise it?

You might consider some or all of the following: schools, local press and radio, church newspapers and magazines, parent and toddler groups, asylum seeker groups, children's centres, your own church families (encouraging them to bring friends along), posters in local shops or flyers in the library. It's also essential to communicate enthusiastically. One reason the numbers were low in one of our venues at the start of the week was that the team had never done anything like it before and were somewhat suspicious about the concept, which may well have discouraged any families they told about it.

Should we charge?

It's up to you. We charged £1.00 per family per day, which nowhere near covered the costs but was intended to help people who prebooked to commit to turning up. I think a donations pot is much healthier than charging, so that people can give according to their means and their gratitude and no one feels that they're paying for a service. It says something about the church's generosity to do it for free, but if you need to know what money is coming in, by all means make a set charge.

How much will it cost?

Estimate how many people will come, then work out the meal cost per person. Then add, say, £2.00 for craft/extreme skills materials per person per day. There are other costs—including decorations, staff time, photocopying, heating, lighting, publicity, building hire, drinks and biscuits—which you may want to cover.

Is there a logo?

You can download the Messy Family Fun logo from **www.messychurch.org.uk/9781857463050/** and use it with the provisos that apply to the main Messy Church logo, available on the website at **www.messychurch.org.uk/resources/logo/**.

Does the team need a DBS (formerly known as CRB) check?

Check with your denomination's Safeguarding Officer. Ask specifically about the week's team and about occasional visitors who come to lead a one-off activity or skill.

Can we run the club without providing a meal?

Think seriously about the reasons why you would offer a meal at a normal Messy Church. If it seems worthwhile, in terms of the social benefits and of what it tells people about church, have a meal at the Messy Family Fun Club too. For us, it was a given, even though neither of the venues was ideally equipped for serving food.

Five-day

Messy Family Fun

Club

*

Overview of the week

Our week's theme was, quite simply, Jesus. The five consecutive days meant that we could build up a picture of him using well-known stories. We felt that, although we were looking at up to ten different stories about Jesus every day, this wouldn't be confusing, as so many of the stories were familiar to the families, at least in broad-brush terms. Stories could be told briefly at the activity tables and the MC could explore one in greater depth during the celebration at the end of the morning.

We aimed to remind people of what they already knew and throw in some stories that they might have forgotten or never encountered. We covered a great deal, but you can learn a lot when you're having fun. One grandmother on the team said she was amazed at how much her eight-year-old granddaughter had learned during the day as she chatted about it at home in the evening.

Day 1: Jesus' stories

The familiar, funny, friendly, superficially non-threatening nature of the parables is a good place to start when families are coming into a strange environment on the first day. It gives them gentle stories and themes to start with, however subversive the parables may be when you dig a little deeper.

Day 2: Jesus' friends

Jesus was fully human and was surrounded by friends who offer us models of discipleship (as well as anti-models, showing us what not to do). Again, many of the names and stories may be familiar, though somewhat buried in the memory banks. These accounts of how Jesus related to the people around him show us his priorities and preoccupations. Through the way he treated his friends, we start to see what sort of a person he was himself.

Day 3: Jesus' miracles

Jesus was also fully God, and halfway through the week we see him doing things that disturb our expectations and evoke awe and wonder. We start moving into the more obvious examples of the supernatural in his life.

Day 4: Jesus and prayer

Jesus' most important relationship was the one he had with his Father, and he worked on this relationship through prayer. In this session we explore what prayer is and how to do it.

Day 5: Jesus dies and rises again

Our Messy Family Fun Club was held at Easter, so it made perfect sense for us to explore the Good Friday/Easter story and take the festival to a level beyond chocolate. At any other time of year, the impact might be even greater as families start to make the link between the commercial Easter that they experienced months ago and the real celebration. The whole of Jesus' life—his stories, miracles and dealings with others—comes to a climax in this one great act of power and love.

*

Day 1: Jesus' stories

Preparation for activity time

Read this out to the team:

Today we look at some of the best-known stories of Jesus as a way of helping families feel that they are coming to the Messy Family Fun Club with some knowledge. Even if they can't remember any details, they may have a faint memory of stories like the good Samaritan or the lost sheep. They are also stories that parents want their children to know for 'general knowledge'. Don't worry if you only get a chance to give a fleeting glimpse of each story: today is broad brush rather than fine detail. We're trying to help families to feel that these stories belong to them, to enthuse people with an interest in the stories, a sense that they're fun and that the person who told them—Jesus— is a great person to know.

Have a copy of each story printed out in large print on the relevant table so that people who want to can read it as they do the activity, and so that team members can remind themselves of the story beforehand.

It is also worth spending a short time beforehand giving team members an opportunity to tell the story in their own words in an abbreviated form as a rehearsal for when the families arrive.

Welcome chill time

Key words: Hands and fingers

The church is full of stories; *you* are full of stories; we *all* like stories.

Writers use their fingers to type or write stories, so warm up your fingers and hands. *(Wave, touch, massage, shake, play the piano, play air guitar)*

We use our hands to write with, and some people use their hands to tell stories with. There are lots of different ways of greeting people with our hands, too. Let's try them out. *(High five, wave, respect)*

There are all sorts of stories. I'm going to call out different types of story, and if this is your favourite, wave your hands and then gather in groups and greet the people there with one of these hand greetings. *(Horror stories, adventure stories, romantic stories, science fiction stories, fairy stories, real-life stories, travel stories, animal stories)*

And then there are Bible stories. *(Bring out the big Bible box.)* Jesus was a great storyteller. There are all sorts of stories to explore today: donkey stories, runaway stories, sheep stories, money stories, impossible stories, digging stories, amazing stories, food stories, building stories and growing stories. So, as we go and enjoy the different activities today, let's see which of Jesus' stories we find out about.

Gathering

We used this every day as the welcome song:

• 'Welcome, everybody' (Fischy Music)

Activities

Donkey balloon racing

LUKE 10:25–37

You will need

Balloons; smooth string; drinking straws; tape; paper; scissors; marker pen

Cut out two pointy ears from the paper and tape them to an uninflated balloon. Draw on eyes with the marker pen. Tape a 5–10 cm length of drinking straw on to the balloon, behind the ears, and thread string through the straw. You can either tie one end of the string to a table leg and hold the other or hold both ends and pull the string tight. Blow up the balloon and let it fly jet-propelled along the string. Race donkeys against each other.

Talk about the story of the good Samaritan and the kind man who put the injured traveller on his own donkey. Jesus wanted people to help others, however different they were from each other.

Health and safety

Hold the string up where no one will run into it, and guard your balloons from small people trying to blow up every single one.

Pig biscuits

LUKE 15:11–32

Option 1

You will need

Hand wipes; paper plates; knives; spoons; Rich Tea biscuits; bowl of big marshmallows; bowl of small marshmallows; bowl of icing (for glue); chocolate spread or brown icing; chocolate mint sticks

Cover a biscuit with chocolate spread or brown icing for pig muck. Make a pig out of one big marshmallow and one little one, glued together with icing, and use chocolate mint sticks for the pen walls. Alternatively, give people free rein to design their own version. Eat as soon as made!

Tell the story of the prodigal son and talk about how horrible it must have been for the boy to work with the pigs. The father in the story loved him even though he'd made such bad decisions.

Option 2

You will need

Biscuit dough (made using the instructions below); extra flour; rolling pins; circle cutters; knives; chocolate drops or chips; baking trays; baking parchment; wire racks; spatula; access to oven

Make up a batch of biscuit dough by stirring together 225 g self-raising flour and 100 g caster sugar. Rub in 85 g margarine, add one beaten egg and knead gently.

Give each person a small portion of dough to roll out on a floury surface. Cut out a large circle as the face. Cut a smaller circle as the nose and place it in the centre of the face. Poke two holes for nostrils. Cut two triangular ears and place them suitably. Place the biscuit on baking parchment on the baking tray, making sure the parchment shows the name of the person who has made the biscuit.

Bake at 180°C/Gas Mark 4 for about ten minutes or until golden brown. Cool on a rack, adding two chocolate drops or chips for eyes while still warm. (If desired, you could also make a pig's bottom of the same size, with a curly tail on it.)

Pigs' dinner

LUKE 15:11–32

You will need

Chocolate dip made from Fairtrade chocolate melted beforehand and mixed with single cream; fresh fruit cut into small pieces; cocktail sticks

Put the dip into a rustic-looking bowl or a container you've made to resemble a trough. Invite people to dip some fruit in, and enjoy your pigs' meal.

Clean hands before and after any activity that involves food.

Sheep badges

LUKE 15:1–7

Option 1

You will need

Card; circle template and head-shape template; scissors; pencils; circular cotton wool pads; black funky foam in squares; googly eyes; safety pins; glue; sticky tape

Make a badge from a cotton wool pad glued on to a circle of card. Cut out a sheep head shape from the funky foam and glue it on. Add googly eyes. Tape a safety pin on to the back.

Tell the story of the lost sheep. Make the link with the story of the lost son (see the pig biscuits above) and talk about how much the shepherd loved the one sheep. Have you ever felt lost? Link this story to the prayer station ideas on page 28.

Option 2

You will need

Black pipe cleaners; coloured wool; tape; safety pin; needle and thread

Bend the pipe cleaners into a little sheep shape. Wrap the wool round and round it, quite tightly, to make a 'fleece'. When the sheep is as fat as you want it to be and just the head and legs are sticking out, secure the wool with tape or by threading the loose end underneath the rest of the wool. Tape or sew a safety pin on the back.

Beware of pinpricks with younger children.

Coin purse

LUKE 15:8–10

This craft is really easy when you've seen the model, and adults love doing it. (Thanks to our Messy Aussie friends!)

You will need

Clean one-litre fruit juice carton (the tall thin ones are best, but the squarer ones are fine); scissors; stick-on Velcro; 5p coins; coloured electrical tape

Cut the top and bottom off the carton (best done beforehand as this removes a stage of explanation and also gives the carton a chance to dry out completely). Collapse the sides to flatten it, then fold it into thirds from top to bottom. On the top third, trim off three of the four sides to leave a flap. Cover the raw edges with coloured tape. Fold the bottom two-thirds up against each other and put a square of stick-on Velcro to hold it together in the centre. Fold down the flap over the whole purse and add another square of Velcro on each surface to hold the flap down. Put in one 5p piece.

Tell the story of the woman with the ten silver coins and link to the other 'lost' parables. How do you know how much the woman wanted to find her lost coin?

Simpler version

Younger people might try this simpler option while their adult grapples with the one above.

You will need

Old coloured envelopes; sticky tape; stick-on Velcro; stickers; coloured pens

Simply seal the envelope, then fold it into thirds. Lift up the top third: this will be the flap. To make the 'pocket' of the purse (the bit that will hold your money) tape up the sides of the lower two thirds, which are lying flat against each other with the fold at the bottom. Stick on squares of Velcro to hold the flap shut against the pocket. Decorate with stickers and pens.

Mini mosaics

MATTHEW 13:44–46

You will need

Mosaic kits from Infinite Crafts (www.inf.co.uk/infinite/Messy-Church-Mini-Mosaics-KM0003.html)

Make up the mosaic crosses according to the kit.

Tell the story of the man who found buried treasure. What do you think the story means? Link this story to the prayer station ideas on page 28.

 Health and safety The mosaic squares could present a swallowing hazard for babies and young children.

Budget version

You will need

Very simple outline picture of a treasure chest; old coloured magazines; scissors; glue

Cut blocks of colour from the magazine pages into small squares and glue on to the treasure chest to make a paper mosaic.

Story bags

You will need

Plain paper bags (such as Chinese takeaway bags); stencils; paint in trays; potato print shapes or foam stampers in the shape of things from today's stories (sheep, coins, crosses, seeds, pigs, donkeys); the Messy Family Fun logo printed on to sticky labels

Decorate a bag to hold all today's story crafts. When you take them home and pull them out one by one, see if you can tell Jesus' stories to someone who wasn't here.

 Tip You could include this activity on every day of the club, but encourage people to reuse their bag rather than making a new one.

Banqueting table mats

LUKE 14:15–23

You will need

Glue; collage shapes; sequins; stickers; felt tips; print-outs of the table mat template from page 79; laminator and pouches

Decorate the table mat around the words of the grace. Laminate it.

Tell the story of the great banquet.

 Health and safety Keep people away from the hot laminator. Make sure the cable isn't a trip hazard. Don't put 3D shapes on to the paper base.

See appendices

Table mat template (page 79)

Giant tree

MATTHEW 13:31–32

You will need

A sturdy base (a pot filled with sand or similar); plenty of cardboard tubes of all sizes; a lot of duct tape; green paper for leaves; scissors; pencils; old tights; newspapers; feathers; googly eyes; yellow funky foam or felt for beaks

Junk model the biggest tree you can with tubes, tape, green paper leaves and rolls of newspaper. The ends of the tubes and newspaper rolls can be fringed to look more attractive.

Make a bird to sit in the tree, from a pair of tights cut off at the foot, rolled back on itself and stuffed with newspaper. Glue on feathers, a funky foam beak and googly eyes.

Tell the story of the mustard seed. Link the story to the prayer station idea below.

Building on jelly

MATTHEW 7:24–27

You will need

Large bowls of ready-set jelly (not too solid, about three pints in each); toy building bricks

See how high you can build with toy bricks in the bowl of jelly while someone shakes the bowl gently.

Tell the story of the two builders.

Discourage people from eating the jelly.

Shaving foam marbling

MATTHEW 18:21–35

You will need

Shaving foam; newspapers; food colouring or liquid paint; spoon for swirling; paper; bin bags

Squirt shaving foam on to a sheet of newspaper. Drop food colouring on top and swirl with a spoon. Place paper over it and press down to print messily. What a mess on the table!

Tell the story of the unforgiving servant and talk about what a mess the servant made of the situation by not forgiving his friend.

Different brands of shaving foam last different lengths of time in this activity. It's worth experimenting beforehand to see how much you'll need.

Prayer station ideas

Station 1

You will need

Green paper or fabric; lolly sticks or similar; model sheep

Create a sheep pen out of lolly sticks on a green field and have some model sheep scattered around. Invite people to put the sheep back in the pen with the others. Thank God for loving you as much as a shepherd loves his sheep.

Station 2

You will need

Chocolate coins; decorative box; colourful fabric

Place the coins in a treasure chest, half-hidden by a swirled sheet of fabric. Eat *one* chocolate coin and ask God to help you find real treasure in your life.

Station 3

You will need

Seeds in a dish

Invite people to pick up some seeds, feel how tiny they are and think what they might grow into. Ask God to turn your life into something unimaginably wonderful for him.

Celebration: The sower

If you've got eyes, get seeing,
If you've got hands, then do,
If you've got ears, then listen,
This story's one for you.

(To the tune of Old Macdonald, believe it or not)

Old Macdonald had a farm,
Ee-i-ee-i-o.
And on that farm he had some seed,
It was time to sow.

He poured the seed into his bag,
Took it to his field,
'Oo-arr,' he said, 'think of the bread
That all this seed will yield!'

And on that field there was a path,
Ee-i-ee-i-o.
He dropped some seed upon that path
But before it started to grow…

(To a bouncy beat)

There came a circus parade with fifteen elephants,
A troupe of ballerinas who all began to dance,
Thirty kids from Padnell* School in football boots and trainers
And half the Roman Army on their way to Venezuela…

As well as…

(To the tune of Sing a Song of Sixpence)

Four and twenty blackbirds, blue and red birds too,
Half a dozen ostrich escaped from London Zoo,
A flock of hungry seagulls, a budgie going tweet
And Old Macdonald's chickens who all wanted lots to eat.

And the seed on the path got…

(To a sad beat)

Trampled on and trodden on
And squidged and squelched and gobbled on
And pecked at and poked at and kicked off and squashed flat
Until it was all gone.

All together now… Aaah.

So Old Macdonald threw seed around,
Ee-i-ee-i-o.
And this seed fell on rocky ground
And this seed started to grow.

(To a rock beat)

'Cos it could rock (dum dum dum dum),
Oh yes it could rock (dum dum dum dum),
Threw down its roots and threw up its shoots
On the rock.
Stone the crows! Yeah!

(Sadly)

But it was dry on the rock and it wasn't very earthy
And the little tiny seedlings soon felt very thirsty
And one by one
They shrivelled up and died.

All together now… Aaaah.

So Old Macdonald sowed some more,
Ee-i-ee-i-o.
And this seed looked all right for sure,
Ee-i-ee-i-o.

But little did Old Macdonald know…

(Theme from 'Jaws')

That there in the ground already
(Jaws noise)
Were lurking the seeds of
(Jaws noise)
Thornbushes!!!!
(Jaws noise)
That grew up and strangled the poor little plants.
Urggggh!

All together now… Aaaaah.

(Very slow and tragically sad)

So Old Macdonald's seeds were sown,
Ee-i-ee-i-o.
And not a single one was grown…
Ee-i-just a mo…

Except…
The seeds that fell in the good ground!

* or whatever school you like!

(Very cheerily, to the tune of 'In An English Country Garden')

Strong healthy stalks and bushy shiny leaves
From the seed that fell on good ground.
Non-G.M., organic and resistant to disease,
The seed that fell in good ground.
Look at it! It grew and grew!
Miles of it, not just a few,
See it waving in the breeze!
There was flour for pies and poppadums and pancakes and for pasties
From the seed that fell in good ground.

Follow up the story with a reflection that Jesus' stories were scattered like the farmer's seeds in the minds of the people who listened to them.

We're still listening to those stories today. Are we going to just let them bounce away like seeds on the path, by forgetting them? Or are we going to try to help each other to remember them and wonder about what they mean, so that they settle into our lives like the seeds in the good ground?

• Song suggestion: 'Written on the palm of God's hand' (Fischy Music)

Prayer

Use different hand positions for each line of the prayer.

Jesus told stories of forgiveness. Help us to forgive others.
    (Hand position: letting go)
He told stories of searching. Help us to value others.
    (Hand position: holding close)
He told stories of challenge. Help us to care about others.
    (Hand position: welcoming)

Messy Grace

May the grace of our Lord Jesus Christ
    (Hold out your hands as if expecting a present)
and the love of God
    (Put your hands on your heart)
and the fellowship of the Holy Spirit
    (Hold hands)
be with us all now and for ever. Amen!
    (Raise hands together on the word 'Amen')

• Song suggestion: 'As we go now' (Fischy Music)

*

Day 2: Jesus' friends

Preparation for activity time

The sweep of today's stories is as broad as yesterday's, with a focus of what it means to be a friend of Jesus today as well. The stories include a mixture of friends, old and young, men and women, healthy and needy.

Read this out to the team:

Today we look at some more well-known stories—this time some of the ones about Jesus' friends. There's an emphasis on Jesus seeking out very ordinary people to be his friends. He loves them just as they are, but meeting Jesus also usually means changing and becoming more like him in some way. All ages understand something about friendship and we'll encourage them to think also about their own friends and to pray for them.

Welcome chill time

Key word: Faces

We have best friends who have friendly faces; we make friends, keep friends and find friends. So today we're going to warm up with face movements. *(Smiles, laughs, eyebrows raised, blowing kisses, surprised faces, excited faces)*

First impressions are so important. Let's get moving!

- Find a friend who is exactly the same height as you.
- Find a friend who wears exactly the same colour clothes as you.
- Find a friend who is exactly the same age as you.
- Find a friend who takes the same shoe size as you.
- Find a friend who loves dogs/cats/Dr Who/ football…
- Find a friend who was born in the same month as you.
- Now find a friend who is as different as possible from you in size, age, likes, birthday month, hair colour (and so on).

Jesus had friends of all sorts, and some of his friends were quite a surprise. Today we'll learn about his close friends and also some secret friends, some dubious friends, some wild friends, some loyal friends, some loud friends, some quiet friends, some busy friends, some greedy friends and some surprise friends. Enjoy!

Gathering

- Song suggestion: 'Welcome, everybody'

Activities

Fishing crew

MATTHEW 4:18–22

Clay fishermen

> **You will need**
>
> Airdrying clay; tools; a model boat (the size of a remote-controlled type); a pre-made clay figure to represent Jesus in the boat

Make a 5–10 cm high figure of yourself out of the clay and add it to the crew in the boat with Jesus.

Talk about the way Jesus invited ordinary fishermen (Simon Peter, Andrew, James and John) to be his friends and gave them a really important job to do: fishing for people instead of fish. Jesus carries on calling ordinary people like us today to be his friends.

Cardboard fishing scene

You will need

A very large cardboard boat profile (sideways on); lots of carpet roll inner tubes; pens; wool; coloured paper; cloth scraps; scissors; glue; one prepared tube to represent Jesus

Encourage everyone to make an 'avatar' of themselves from a carpet tube decorated with woolly hair, stuck-on paper eyes and so on, and stand it behind the boat frontage. This is a great photo opportunity to stand in the boat with 'Jesus' and 'yourself'.

Money box

LUKE 19:1–10

You will need

Cocoa tins, pots, jars and similar, with lids; old magazines; stickers; scissors; glue; glue spreaders

Beforehand, prepare each container lid by cutting a slit big enough for coins to go through.

Decorate a container with collage scraps from magazines to make a money box. A coat of watery PVA glue makes a good substitute for varnish.

Zacchaeus was in love with money until Jesus called him; then he saw what was even more important. What will you spend your money on? How much are you willing to share with others who need it?

'Give her something to eat' butty

MARK 5:21–43

You will need

A variety of breads, spreads and fillings, with some weird and wacky ones alongside the more predictable ones; plates; knives; spoons; hand wipes

Suggestions for fillings include chocolate spread, jam, Fairtrade honey, pickle, cheese, soft cheese, ham, squirty mustard, mayonnaise, pâté, squirty cream and hummus.

Make the perfect (or the worst ever) sandwich. The only proviso is that you have to eat what you've made.

Jesus brought a girl back from the dead and told her parents to give her something to eat.

Tip

You could have the DVD of *The Miracle Maker* playing nearby, as it tells the story of Jesus from the little girl's point of view.

Health and safety

Make sure hands are clean. Check for allergies. Check that the chocolate spread does not include nuts.

Secret messages

JOHN 3:1–21

Option 1

You will need

White candles or white wax crayons; white paper; watery black paint; wide brushes

Write a secret message for someone to discover. Write or draw using white wax and let someone else paint over it with watery black paint to reveal the message.

Option 2

You will need

Offcuts of fur fabric; thin elastic; black card or thick paper; spectacles template (see page 80); scissors; glue; a stapler; pencils

Make disguises using false beards and moustaches held on by elastic, dark glasses, eye patches, top hats or a square of black paper licked and stuck on a tooth to give a lovely 'missing tooth' effect.

Nicodemus wanted to follow Jesus but started by doing it secretly, just as our white wax messages start secret, or as our disguises hide the real person's face from view.

See appendices

Spectacles template (page 80)

Volcano

LUKE 10:38–42

You will need

A pot with a narrow opening; a funnel or cone of paper; tray; vinegar; bicarbonate of soda; red food colouring or watery red paint; spoons; a bucket for waste

Make a volcano erupt: using the funnel, add vinegar to bicarbonate of soda and red food colouring contained within a pot on a tray.

Extreme version

Thanks to Locks Heath Free Church for this idea.

You will need

Small plastic bags with strong seals; bicarbonate of soda; paper towels; vinegar; a funnel; a bucket; tongs; safety goggles

First, put vinegar in a plastic bag. Place bicarbonate of soda on an open paper towel and fold it to make a loose parcel, small enough to fit inside the bag. Then put the paper towel into the bag, quickly seal the bag and place it in a large bucket or bowl, or use a long-handled pair of tongs to hold it at a distance. Shake it up so that the vinegar gets to the bicarbonate. The bag should pop and the contents fizz out more or less dramatically.

Martha was Jesus' friend. She wanted to follow Jesus but she was very angry and erupted like a volcano because her sister didn't help with all the work that needed doing. She had to learn to listen to Jesus.

 Wear safety goggles.

Loo-roll wrapping

JOHN 11:1–44

You will need

Lots of loo roll

Wrap someone from your family in loo roll to look like grave clothes. You could compete with another family for the best-wrapped body.

Jesus cared deeply when his friend Lazarus, who was Martha and Mary's brother, died. He made him come back to life. How amazing to have a friend like Jesus!

River Jordan

MATTHEW 3:1–17

Option 1

You will need

A large piece of paper, ideally light blue, with symbolic waves drawn on it; felt tips or wax crayons

Lie down on the paper and ask a friend or family member to draw round your body. Then decorate 'yourself' with a swimsuit or ordinary clothes, face, hair and so on.

Option 2

You will need

Floor covering (or do the activity outside); plenty of aluminium foil; water; junk to make bridges and boats; dolls to represent John, soldiers and others in the story

Make a river by unrolling the foil, turning up each long side about 4 cm to make a channel, then pouring water down it from one end. Give families the chance to landscape their rivers, join one to another, build bridges, get wet and play at the John the Baptist story or other soggy games.

John the Baptist was Jesus' friend. He told everyone they needed to get ready for Jesus by getting baptised, or washed, in the river to make a new start. Even today, people who want to show they are Jesus' friends get baptised.

Soap making

MARK 1:40–44
(OR YOU COULD USE MANY OTHER STORIES)

You will need

A soap-making kit (available from Infinite Crafts or large craft stores); a microwave; small polythene bags

Make some little soaps according to the instructions in the pack and put them in the bags to take home.

Some of Jesus' friends were people who had had no friends until the time they met him. They had diseases that meant they weren't allowed to live near other people. Jesus healed them and made them clean again so that they could be with the people they loved once more.

Health and safety Be careful with the warm soap mixture. Make sure the cable for the microwave isn't a tripping hazard.

T-shirt decorating

STORIES OF ISAIAH, JEREMIAH, EZRA, JOEL AND SO ON

You will need

Plain T-shirts; fabric pens or paints; an iron and ironing board, or ironing instructions printed out

Decorate a T-shirt. Give out instructions if the T-shirts will need ironing at home.

The prophets who lived many years before Jesus could still be considered his friends, because they told people all about how fantastic he would be. They acted as signposts to Jesus, for other people to see. When people ask us about the T-shirt we've made, we can tell them where we made it and about what we've done at the Messy Family Fun Club.

Health and safety Be careful with the hot iron (adult use only). Make sure the flex for the iron isn't a tripping hazard.

No easy ride

LUKE 9:57–62

You will need

Junk boxes (such as cereal boxes); sticks or dowelling rods; lids to make wheels; sticky tape; glue; prepared stickers, about the length of a cereal box, that say 'No easy rides with Jesus!'

Using boxes, sticks and lids, make a jeep to go on an adventure. Stick the stickers along the sides.

Jesus never promised his friends an easy ride. In fact, he said it would be hard to follow him and his friends would have a difficult time. Even today, it's never easy to follow him. I wonder why people still do it?

Prayer station ideas

Station 1

You will need

A ground covering of nice fabric; an upright cross; wooden or paper people

Place a paper person on the ground covering, close to or far from the cross to show how near you feel to Jesus at the moment. You could ask Jesus to help you come nearer to him this week.

Station 2

You will need

Map pins; tiny sticky notes; metallic thread (or coloured wool); a large corkboard or sheet of corrugated card; pens

Prepare the board by sticking some of the pins into the centre to make a cross shape.

Families write or draw a friend's name or picture on a tiny sticky note and stick it to a pin. Do this for as many friends as you like. Write one for yourself too. Stick the pins in the board. Pray for your friends by tying one end of the thread to the cross, then winding it slowly round each friend's pin in turn, asking Jesus to bless that friend as you do so.

Station 3

You will need

A selection of lighted incense burners or essential oils dropped into bowls of water, or a selection of different scented soaps; towels; cotton wool swabs; a print-out of Proverbs 27:9 (below).

Invite people to come and smell the perfumes. Talk about how they make you feel and which smells make you feel relaxed and refreshed. Talk about the words from Proverbs and which of your friends make you happy. Take away a swab doused in the perfume you prefer. When you sniff it, thank God for those friends and for Jesus, who wants to be our friend.

The sweet smell of incense can make you feel good, but true friendship is better still.

PROVERBS 27:9

Celebration

Story

Retell the story of Zacchaeus (Luke 19:1–10), acting it out together. As you read the story, have a Zacchaeus, a Jesus and a set of 'good people' from Jericho to mime the actions, with everyone else as members of the crowd adding boos for Zacchaeus and cheers for Jesus. Encourage your actors to improvise as you tell the story. A chair can be used as a tree if you hold Zacchaeus' hand to keep him/her safe.

Afterwards, ask the families to decide what they like best about Jesus in this story. Talk together about their responses.

There is also a rhyming version of this story in *The Gospels Unplugged* (Barnabas for Children, 2011).

• Song suggestion: 'Written on the palm of God's hand' (Fischy Music)

Prayer

Make a face shape by making a circle with your hands. Start with a small circle, then a larger circle, and then a very large one as you pray for different circles of friendships in our lives. Let's pray for the people who are our best friends... the people who live in the same place, whom we might see on the bus and in the street... people all over this country in other towns and cities... and people all round the world.

Messy Grace

May the grace of our Lord Jesus Christ
    (Hold out your hands as if expecting a present)
and the love of God
    (Put your hands on your heart)
and the fellowship of the Holy Spirit
    (Hold hands)
be with us all now and for ever. Amen!
    (Raise hands together on the word 'Amen')

• Song suggestion: 'You are a star' (Fischy Music)

*

Day 3: Jesus' miracles

Preparation for activity time

We home in on Jesus as a powerful person—the 'fully God' side of his nature—and enjoy exploring some of the amazing things he did. Again, many of these are stories that people may know, at least in part.

Read this out to the team:

Today we're looking at Jesus' power as the Son of God. It would be a good idea to think for a moment now about which of his miracles makes you go 'Wow!' Tell the person next to you. Can you communicate some of that excitement and awe to the families who come today?

Welcome chill time

Key word: Feet

We need to use our feet today to explore some amazing changes that happened when people came close to Jesus and Jesus came close to them.

- Wave a foot, wiggle a toe, dance, line dance, and walk on the edges of your feet, on your heels and on your toes.
- Try some tightrope walking, standing on one foot, hopping, jumping and walking with your feet stuck together.
- Try slow-motion running, backwards running, walking together joined at the ankles.
- Play 'Walk this way': follow a leader in groups of threes and fours.
- With friends, link up your left feet in twos and then in groups of four, eight and sixteen.

Jesus got people walking who couldn't walk before. Some walked on water; some found dancing feet at a wedding; some ran to tell others the good news; and some were rooted to the spot in amazement. Let's go and find out about this amazing man.

Gathering

- Song suggestion: 'Welcome, everybody'

Activities

Walk on the waves challenge

MATTHEW 14:22–36

You will need

A large blue or green tarpaulin or length of fabric; blue or green footprint shapes; bubble blowing facilities; a water pistol; water

Place the footprint shapes along the length of fabric so that there is a certain amount of difficulty in getting from one to the other. Challenge people to walk on the water, staying only on the footprints and dodging the 'sea spray'—the bubbles you blow at them to represent the storm. If you're outside, you might shoot at people with a water pistol or spray gun too, depending on their age and tolerance for getting wet. Describe how Jesus walked on water and invited Peter to join him.

If you have a link with a water charity, this might be an opportunity to talk about people who have to walk miles to get water, and to raise some money for the charity with an appropriate activity. For example, you could give out small bottles of water and ask people to bring them back full of money by the end of the week.

Extreme version

If the budget permits, hire some Zorbs (the huge transparent hamster balls) for the day and really walk on water.

Blindfold painting

MARK 10:46–52

You will need

Big sheets of paper; aprons; brushes; paints; blindfolds

Challenge people to paint a picture of something you say (a tree, their mum, themselves, a dog, a butterfly) while blindfolded. Talk about the way Jesus made blind Bartimaeus see again.

Five thousand people

JOHN 6:1–15

You will need

Paint in shallow trays; handwipes; large sheets of paper with hillsides drawn on them; black felt pens

Invite people to make lots and lots of thumbprints in paint over the hillsides. They might also add faces and limbs to the thumbprints that have already dried, using the felt pens. Talk about the time Jesus fed over 5000 people with the bread and fish from a little boy's picnic lunch.

This is an opportunity to talk about working miracles to change people's lives and feed the hungry through organisations such as Christian Aid. You might follow up in a Messy Church session by using one of the 'justice' Messy Church session outlines written with Christian Aid, Operation Christmas Child or the Children's Society.

Variations

Use potato prints or sponge prints, or glue dried breadcrumbs over an outline picture of Jesus performing this miracle and make a border of little fish.

Wine-glass painting

JOHN 2:1–11

You will need

Cheap wine glasses; brushes; glass paints (or nail varnish as a cheaper option)

Decorate a wine glass to remember the time Jesus was at a wedding in Cana and turned gallons of water into wine. You could print off some images from the internet for inspiration.

Encourage people to leave the stem free of paint so that it's easier to carry the glass home, and remind them not to put the glass in the dishwasher.

Spaghetti nets

LUKE 5:1–11

You will need

Paper; long spaghetti cooked in a little vegetable oil and allowed to cool (the oil keeps it reasonably flexible when it cools); brushes; paints in shallow trays

Paint a picture of fish swimming. Then drag strings of cooked spaghetti through the paint and across the fish picture to make a coloured net over the fish. Tell the story of the miraculous catch of fish.

Bottle fish

LUKE 5:1–11

You will need

A paddling pool filled with water; small plastic bottles; stickyback plastic; scissors; toy fishing nets

Decorate the bottles with stickyback plastic fins and tails, then throw them in the pool and see how many you can catch in a single net in 30 seconds.

Storms in bottles

MATTHEW 8:23–27

You will need

Small water bottles; vegetable oil; blue or green food colouring; Alka Seltzer tablets

Fill the bottle one-third full of water. Add another one-third of oil and a few drops of food colouring. Drop in a broken-up Alka Seltzer tablet and watch the waters seethe. (At home, the storm can be refreshed by adding more Alka Seltzers.) Talk about the way Jesus calmed the storm when his friends were scared they would drown.

Health and safety

Ensure that parents/carers, not the children, take these bottles home, and explain that they have dangerous medicine in them and are not to be drunk under any circumstances.

Family scrapbooking

LUKE 7:11–16

Invite families to bring in family photos for this activity.

Option 1

You will need

Selection of good-quality papers, stickers, stampers, hole-punches and so on; photos or the means of taking a photo and printing it out there and then

Make a scrapbook page of your family using paper frames, hole-punches, stickers and so on. Jesus knew how important families are: when a woman's son died and she had no one left to look after her, Jesus brought the boy back to life.

Option 2

Make a card to tell someone in your family how much you love them.

Party cocktails

MARK 1:29–34

You will need

Fruit juices; fizzy drinks; drinking straws; small clear plastic cups; drinks umbrellas and any other cocktail gadgetry

Make celebratory fruity cocktails with different fruit juices and fizzy drinks. Jesus healed people so that they could rejoin society; they must have had great parties to celebrate being back together with their families and friends!

House model

LUKE 5:17–26

Option 1

You will need

Cardboard boxes; small boxes (size of mini cereal boxes); scissors; string; dowelling rods; card; pens

Make a house out of a cardboard box with a winding mechanism on the roof that lowers down a little mat.

Lay a cardboard box on its side and cut a hole in the top. Place two small boxes, one on either side of the hole. Push a dowelling rod into each box, so that it extends across the hole. Hang two strings from the rod and attach a mat of paper to the strings. Wind the rod to lower or raise the mat.

Jesus forgave a man's sins and made him walk again.

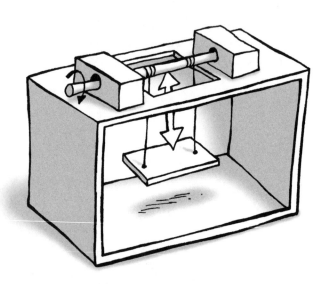

Option 2

You will need

Lots of cardboard boxes; lightweight cardboard tubes; large sheets of lightweight card or paper; shredded paper; a stepladder; Action Man doll or similar

Build a giant house out of the junk. Give it a flat roof from very lightweight materials such as cardboard tubes taped together over sheets of paper, and a 'thatch' of shredded paper. Have a great moment breaking open the roof: if you can see it's safe enough, get as many people as possible inside the house and have one person on a stepladder break through the roof from the outside, showering the people inside with debris. Lower an Action Man down on a string.

 Don't crush anyone or poke their eye out with a falling tube.

Pustulous boils

LUKE 5:12–16

You will need

Water; green, yellow, red and pink tissue paper; petroleum jelly; baby oil; face paint

From the materials provided, make fake wounds on arms or hands. (One group even went so far as to pre-inject the capsules from bubblewrap with green liquid so that they could be incorporated in the wound and popped. But I leave this to your discretion.)

Jesus made people with horrible skin diseases better so that they could become part of society again.

 Check for skin allergies or sensitivities.

Prayer station ideas

Station 1

You will need

A picture of Jesus and the blind man; speech bubble sticky notes; pens

Jesus asked the blind man, 'What do you want me to do for you?' Write this question in a speech bubble above Jesus' head in a large picture of the scene, with the blind man's back to the viewer so that it could be anyone of any age or gender. Invite people to write their reply to his question on a sticky note and stick it on the picture around the blind man.

Station 2

You will need

A DVD playing (or a clearly illustrated printed story) of a family in a difficult situation who are finding a way out of it (see the Christian Aid or Tearfund resources online); two sheets of paper for people to draw on, one labelled 'Thank you, God, for…' and one labelled 'Please, God…'

Families can leave a prayer response to the story they hear or read about.

Station 3

You will need

Duplo® or similar and the start of a model

Add a brick on to the model and think about the way that it can grow and grow if everybody adds just one piece at a time. How can we work miracles together to make great things grow in the world?

Celebration

Story

Act out together the story of the man being lowered through the roof from Luke 5:17–26. Choose actors to play Jesus, the man on the mat and the four friends. Everyone else is either a crowd member or a teacher of the law, as they choose. Crowd members can practise saying, 'Ooh, this Jesus!' in a wondering, marvelling way, and teachers can practise saying, 'Ooh, this Jesus!' in a critical, carping way, perhaps with a shake of the head.

A few days later, when Jesus again entered Capernaum, the people heard that he had come home.

Invite Jesus to come and sit down in a space that is the imaginary house.

They gathered in such large numbers that there was no room left, not even outside the door…

Memebers of the crowd and the teachers gather round as closely as they can, saying their line to each other.

… and Jesus preached the word to them.

Encourage Jesus to tell some stories from yesterday's Family Fun session, if he can remember one or two.

Some men came, bringing to him a paralysed man, carried by four of them.

If you can do it safely, lay the man on a sturdy blanket carried by four friends. If you fear for the safety of your man, simply have them escort him in, propping him up on their shoulders.

Since they could not get him to Jesus because of the crowd, they made an opening in the roof above Jesus by digging through it, and then lowered the mat the man was lying on.

Encourage your actors to act this out to one side of Jesus and the crowd. Bring the man to lie in front of Jesus.

When Jesus saw their faith, he said to the paralysed man, 'Son, your sins are forgiven.'

Get Jesus to repeat these words. Encourage your crowd to say, 'Ooh, this Jesus!'

Now some teachers of the law were sitting there, thinking to themselves, 'Why does this fellow talk like that? He's blaspheming! Who can forgive sins but God alone?'

Get your teachers to repeat one line each of these words, or, if they are younger, just the critical 'Ooh, this Jesus!'

Immediately Jesus knew in his spirit that this was what they were thinking in their hearts, and he said to them, 'Why are you thinking these things? Which is easier: to say to this paralysed man, "Your sins are forgiven" or to say, "Get up, take your mat and walk"? But I want you to know that the Son of Man has authority on earth to forgive sins.' So he said to the man, 'I tell you, get up, take your mat and go home.'

Have Jesus mime as you read these words.

He got up, took his mat and walked out in full view of them all.

The man does so.

This amazed everyone and they praised God, saying, 'We have never seen anything like this!'

End with choruses of 'Ooh, this Jesus!'

Read the story through again without the actions and ask everyone to notice which word or sentence jumps out at them or seems interesting in some way. Sometimes that's the Holy Spirit showing us something he wants us to think about and remember.

There is also a rhyming version of this story in *The Gospels Unplugged* (Barnabas for Children, 2011).

- Song suggestion: 'Even before I was born' (Fischy Music)

Prayer

Sit down next to someone who is a new friend.

Place your left foot close to the other person's right foot and notice the differences. We pray for those who are different from us and thank God for the way he's made us unique.

Touch heels and pray for those who need healing.

Touch soles and pray for your own inner strength to do the right thing, knowing that God knows every step we take.

Messy Grace

May the grace of our Lord Jesus Christ
  (Hold out your hands as if expecting a present)
and the love of God
  (Put your hands on your heart)
and the fellowship of the Holy Spirit
  (Hold hands)
be with us all now and for ever. Amen!
  (Raise hands together on the word 'Amen')

- Song suggestion: 'Down to earth' (Fischy Music)

*

Day 4: Jesus and prayer

Preparation for activity time

At the Portsmouth Messy Family Fun Club, we used the session on the Lord's Prayer from pages 87–95 of the book *Messy Church 3*, as we felt that, for us, the Lord's Prayer was most important to focus on. Rather than duplicate the whole session here, I've suggested ten different activities on the theme of prayer in general, so consider the ones in *Messy Church 3* Session 6 as alternatives if you wish to concentrate, as we did, on the Lord's Prayer itself.

Read out to the team:

The heartbeat of Jesus' life was his relationship with his heavenly Father, and Jesus prayed in all sorts of ways and at all sorts of times to him. Whatever we believe about prayer, a good reason to pray is because Jesus did. Tell the person next to you about a time when God answered your prayer. Pray now that the families will enjoy praying more as a result of today.

Welcome chill time

Key word: Voices

There are sounds everywhere. This cathedral [or this church] and the world are full of sounds: what can you hear if we're very quiet for a moment?

(Make sounds for clocks ticking, hearts beating, people humming, birds singing, cars hooting, bicycle bells ringing, people shouting, people whispering, doors slamming, doors creaking open, dogs barking, cats miaowing, police cars wailing and babies crying.)

There are always people talking and people listening. Jesus spent time talking and listening to God: he kept close to his Father.

Space yourselves out and call out your favourite colour, speaking and listening to find those who have the same favourite colour as you. Do the same with your favourite TV programme, your favourite food or your favourite place in this town.

Talking and listening to God is prayer. Jesus taught us all about it—where to go, what to say, what to pray, when to pray, how to pray and why to pray. Let's go and explore more about what he meant.

Gathering

- Song suggestion: 'Welcome, everybody'

Activities

String telephones

MATTHEW 6:5–14

You will need

Paper cups; string (about 20 metres per couple of people); a tool to make a hole in the base of the cups

Take two cups and make a hole in the base of each. Thread the string through the holes and knot with large bulky knots to secure. Pull the string tight between the two cups and place one person at each end. One speaks into their cup while the other listens. Experiment with how far away you can get for it still to work.

Talk about how, if you have a mobile phone, you can talk to someone else with a mobile at any time. God is always ready to speak to us or listen to us. We don't need anything special, although sometimes special places or words can help.

Prayer cube

MATTHEW 6:5–14

You will need

A cube 'net' printed on card and a few copies pre-cut; pens; stickers; sticky tape

Ask the families what sort of things they would like to pray for and make a list of six. They will then draw or write something that stands for each of those things/people/situations on one side of the cube while it's still flat. Some people may find stickers that will represent those things.

Cut out the cube and tape it together (I find that glue never sticks securely), then practise praying very short prayers, as Jesus invites us to do in Matthew 6: 'When you pray, don't talk on and on as people do who don't know God. They think God likes to hear long prayers' (v. 7).

You could make a giant version of the cube to pray with in celebrations during the week.

See appendices

Cube net template (page 81)

Prayer treasure hunt

You will need

Sheets of clues as below or adapted for your own building; prizes; the letters P, R, A, Y, E and R, each on a separate card; pens

Set up a treasure hunt around the building. The idea could be to explore spots in the building where you might enjoy praying. If you're in a more traditional church, you might place a letter at the font, the altar, the pulpit, a stained-glass window, a side chapel and the door. Or it might be to associate different sorts of prayer with different parts of the room or furniture, so if you're in a modern secular building, you might put a letter at the door, a window, a fire exit, the kitchen, the bin and so on.

Clues

- People pray for new Christians here. *(Font)*
- People pray around this, especially with bread and wine. *(Altar)*
- This shows someone praying in bright colours. *(Stained-glass window)*
- You can shut the door and be quiet to pray in here. *(Chapel or prayer room)*
- This is where we pray that new people will come in and join us. *(Door)*
- Through this we can see the beautiful world God has made. *(Window)*
- This is where the wonderful cooks make our lunch and pray for us. *(Kitchen)*
- This is like where all the bad things go when we say sorry to God. *(Bin)*

Early in the morning clockwork

MARK 1:35

You will need

Tiny screwdrivers; old (broken) clocks and watches; someone confident in engineering or mechanics; craft wire; wire cutters

Mark tells us that Jesus got up very early in the morning to make time to talk to God. Have fun taking apart the clocks carefully and either mending them (if you can) or making miniature sculptures using the clockwork pieces and the craft wire. Use your clock or sculpture as a reminder that you can talk with God at any time of day or night.

Prayer cupboards

MATTHEW 6:6

You will need

Very large cardboard boxes; scissors; marker pens or paint

Jesus said that we should never pray just to impress people. We should go into a room where we can be on our own, shut the door and be private with God. In the houses he would have been used to, that room might have been the tiny broom cupboard!

Cut a door in your box (cut around three sides so that the fourth side is 'hinged') and paint or write on the door 'Private'. Try going in and saying a prayer in the quietness.

Teaspoons

You will need

Plastic teaspoons; permanent markers in three colours; cut-outs of teacups or mugs made in card; coloured pens and stickers; A5 backing card; a stapler

The old aide-memoire of 'tsp' (the abbreviation for 'teaspoon') is a reminder to say 'thank you' prayers, 'sorry' prayers and 'please' prayers. Write one of the three letters on each of three teaspoons. Decorate the teacup or mug shape and staple it around its sides and base to the backing card. Leave the top of the cup or mug shape open as a pocket to hold the three teaspoons (leave enough space to insert the spoons in the pocket). Talk about which prayers are easiest to say and why.

At home, stick the shape to the wall or fridge and pull out a spoon each day to see what sort of prayer to pray.

Prayer ice game

You will need

Lots of pictures that might inspire prayer, such as newspaper pictures of sad situations, nature pictures, food, weather and local landmarks such as schools or pubs; ice cubes made with paint in different colours; a plank; a roll of narrow paper; glue; foil; a dribble tray; hand wipes

Set up the plank on a gentle slope and make the sides of a channel using the foil. (You could leave out the foil if you don't mind it being a bit messier when the ice cubes fall off the sides.) Roll out the paper down the length of the slope. As a group of people assembles for the activity, ask them to choose one or more of the pictures from your supply and to glue them on the paper. They then take it in turns to release an ice cube at the top of the slope. As their ice cube slithers over each of the pictures, the group says a prayer based on that picture. The ice cubes will leave a rainbow effect on the paper over the top of the pictures.

Talk about how prayer changes situations for the better. You can either throw away the papers or collect them and make them into a display.

Doodle prayers

You will need

Paper; coloured pens; someone artistic and spiritual

Write the name of someone you would like God to bless in the centre of your paper in beautiful letters, then draw a solid line around the name and ask God to protect them. Draw rays coming out from the shape and ask God to bring his light into the person's life. Draw a heart around the whole picture and ask God to show them his love today. Then give everybody space to colour in their doodle and pray for that person in their own way with the different colours and patterns they choose to use.

Hat for a Pharisee

LUKE 18:9–14

You will need

Newspapers; sticky tape; tissue paper and crêpe paper for decorations

Tell the story of the man who thought he was really good and important and the man who knew how bad he was. Talk about the way we come to God in our prayers: are we more like the first man or the second? Talk too about the way that, in times gone by, men and boys would always take off their hats in church or to show respect.

Make a hat that the important man might have worn—a large one with lots of decorations that would make people notice him and think how marvellous he was. Use it as a reminder that when we pray to God, it's a good idea to start by being humble, as if we're 'taking off our hat' to be more like the second man in the story.

Bubble snakes

LUKE 11:11

You will need

Old socks; washing-up liquid; water; plastic bottles with the bases cut off; a bowl

Jesus said that we can trust God to give us good things, not try to trick us, just as a dad wouldn't give us a snake and chips if we asked for fish and chips.

Make a bubble snake. Stretch a sock over the hole at the base of the bottle and dip the sock in the mixture of washing-up liquid and water. Take a deep breath *away* from the bottle, then blow into the mouth of the bottle. A 'snake' of bubbles appears! You can make quite an impressive table full of snakes.

Don't inhale the liquid.

Prayer station idea

As an extra, leave out a shallow tray of sand for people to draw or write prayers in. Shake the tray to erase them.

Celebration

Lord's Prayer actions

Choose twelve people to come and stand at the front, to remember one action each. Explain one action and phrase to each person as you move down the line. If they can't cope with an action and a phrase, they can choose a friend to come and help them.

1) Our Father in heaven	Hold both arms up
2) Hallowed be your name	Make a large circle with both arms in front of you
3) Your kingdom come, your will be done on earth as in heaven	Slowly stretch out your arms to make the shape of Jesus on the cross
4) Give us today our daily bread	Bring your hands together to hold an imaginary loaf
5) Forgive us our sins as we forgive those who sin against us	Mime wiping one hand clean with two strokes of your hand against your palm. Then, for the second phrase, mime wiping the other one clean with four strokes
6) And lead us not into temptation	Cross one arm across your chest
7) But deliver us from evil	Cross the other arm across your chest
8) For the kingdom	Make the outstretched cross shape again
9) the power	Raise your arms like a muscly weight-lifter
10) and the glory	Stretch up high and bring your hands slowly down in front of you, with fingers playing an imaginary piano or imitating raindrops
11) are yours now and for ever	Place your left hand out to your left, then make spiralling shapes going from left to right with your right hand
12) Amen	Clap above your head

Practise going down the line with actions and words. Invite the rest of the group to join in. Go down the line again and ask the actors to do the actions without the words, so that the congregation has to say the words alone. Deliberately miss out some of the people or phrases or jump from one to another in the wrong order.

Play with the prayer in other ways: get the actors moving in a circle, going fast, going slowly, or whatever you are inspired to do.

Ask which is everyone's favourite part. Ask if anything is puzzling. Finish by saying the prayer all together, with actions from everyone.

• Song suggestion: 'Even before I was born', Fischy Music

Prayer

Let's say 'thank you' to God all at once.
Now we'll say 'sorry' to God, all in silence.
Now, just for a moment, we'll listen to God…
And now we all say 'Amen'.

Messy Grace

May the grace of our Lord Jesus Christ
    (Hold out your hands as if expecting a present)
and the love of God
    (Put your hands on your heart)
and the fellowship of the Holy Spirit
    (Hold hands)
be with us all now and for ever. Amen!
    (Raise hands together on the word 'Amen')

• Song suggestion: 'As we go now' (Fischy Music)

Day 5: Jesus dies and rises again

Preparation for activity time

Today we look at Jesus' death and resurrection.

Could I make a plea for avoiding Easter activities that involve bunnies? This was the symbol of the pagan goddess Eostra. You can justify the Christian symbolism of chickens, eggs and chocolate in church, and, if you're running this Messy Family Fun Club around Easter time, people will expect it to involve certain symbols. But let's lose the bunny.

Again, on our Messy Family Fun Club we used Easter activities from previous *Messy Church* books, but here are some different ones.

See also Jane Leadbetter's *Messy Easter* (Messy Church, 2014).

Read this out to the team.

Paul wrote in 1 Corinthians 15:14 that 'if Christ wasn't raised to life, our message is worthless, and so is your faith'. In other words, if Good Friday and Easter Day didn't happen, we've wasted all our time and efforts this week. Today is the day when we have the chance to enjoy this wonderful story again and to share it with people who may have never thought about the meaning of Easter before. Pray that God's Holy Spirit will work in people's hearts as we explore the day that changed everything.

This is a great opportunity to try out one or more of the Infinite Crafts range of Messy Easter kits (Resurrection in a box, Seed eggs, John 3:16 cross, Easter bracelets and Easter cards) at **www.inf.co.uk**.

Welcome chill time

Key words: Whole body

Today everything gets turned inside out and upside down. *(Teach a hand action for this.)*

Let's use our whole body, which is going be affected by today's story:

- Do a total shiver or shake.
- Make everything do circles.
- Be totally still.
- Move so that you can look at the world differently— upside down or from a different angle.

How many cross shapes can you see from where you're standing now? How many can we make on our own? Today we're exploring why some Christians have crosses in churches, wear crosses round their necks and make the sign of the cross when they pray.

In groups of four or five, work together so that everyone is:

- leaning on each other
- holding on to someone else's right knee/left shoulder
- sitting back to back
- standing on one leg
- sitting on bottoms only
- touching, but with two of the group off the ground

Jesus had told great stories, made good friends, done amazing things and taught us helpful ways to know about God, but what would really make a difference? How could people be made new again? Where would the power come from to make a brand new start? Let's go and explore today's amazing story.

Gathering

- Song suggestion: 'Welcome, everybody'

Activities

Story egg box

You will need

Egg boxes for six eggs; print-outs of the six parts of the Easter story; cocktail sticks; general craft supplies

Invite families to make a story box to tell six parts of the Easter story by filling each egg hole with something to stand for each part. They could also decorate the lid of the box.

Give them a print-out of the six story parts:

- Jesus rides into Jerusalem and the crowds wave palm branches to greet him (Luke 19:28–40)
- Jesus eats supper with his friends (Luke 22:7–23)
- Jesus is put on the cross and dies (Luke 23:26–43)
- Jesus is put in a dark tomb (Luke 23:50–56)
- Jesus comes back to life (Luke 24:1–12)
- Now Jesus can be with everyone who asks him (Matthew 28:20)

Dramatic cross

You will need

A large card cross shape stuck on to a larger sheet of paper and then stuck upright on a wall; sponges; dark-coloured paint; aprons; floor covering

Invite people to make a dramatic background for the cross, showing the moment the sky grew dark, by soaking the sponges in paint and throwing them at the sheet of paper from a short distance.

Talk about the dramatic things that happened when Jesus was on the cross—for example, the sky growing dark, the temple curtain ripping in two, and dead people coming out of their graves and walking round the city.

Phone photos of crosses

You will need

Mobile phones with cameras; computer for displaying images

Invite people to go round the building and take photos of all the different sorts of crosses they can find. They might be crucifixes or they might be a cross in a window frame or where two beams meet. They might also be crosses on someone's clothing or in the other activities.

If possible, turn the photos into a montage on the computer and run it during the celebration, with a suitable song playing in the background.

Talk about what you think of when you see a cross shape.

Adventure challenge

You will need

Big junk; torches; lamps; plug boards; sheets; blankets; clothes horses; general craft supplies

Invite people to create a Good Friday to Easter 'journey' course that takes people from the darkness and sadness of Good Friday to the light and joy of Easter. It could be from one end of the building to the other, involving tunnels, caves, secret passages, surprises, scenery and sound effects. They might make one big course together or people might want to make individual ones.

Talk about how sad Jesus' friends were on Good Friday and Saturday, but how amazed they were on Sunday. Talk about the times when we feel despairing. This story gives us hope, however bad things seem.

Shadow puppets

You will need

The ancient OHP that is hiding in a cupboard; a screen; card; scissors; sticky tape; pea sticks

Cut shapes out of card and tape them to the sticks to make scenery and puppets. Then put on a shadow puppet show of some or all of the Easter story. Use the OHP as the light source.

Exploding tomb sculpture

You will need

Nine to 20 bottles coloured with black paint; black duct tape; clean empty two-litre plastic bottles; funnels; white, gold and yellow paint; glitter; bamboo sticks of different lengths; aluminium foil; sticky tape

Make a community sculpture to represent the new life of Jesus bursting out of the darkness of the tomb.

Stand the dark bottles touching each other in a block and use duct tape to tape them together. This makes the base of the sculpture, or represents the tomb.

Using a funnel, pour just enough paint into a two-litre bottle to coat the sides lightly. Use several colours and add glitter. Twist and turn the bottle to make the colours spread and blend. Leave it upside down to dry for a few minutes while you cover a bamboo stick with foil, leaving a 'stopper' of foil at one end to bung up the paint bottle opening (in case of drips) and to hold it steady.

Push the bottle, upside down, on to the end of the bamboo stick and plug the opening with foil. Secure it with tape if necessary. 'Plant' it in one of the black bottles.

As more bright bottles are added, rearrange them at different angles to make the most dynamic and exciting 'explosion' of brightness you can.

Talk about the difference Jesus' resurrection makes.

Cross section

You will need

Ink stampers in the shape of hearts; different coloured inkpads; paper; scissors; glue

Cut out a cross shape from the centre of a sheet of paper and discard it, keeping the paper with the hole in it. (An easy way to do this is to fold the paper in half lengthways and cut out half a cross shape across the fold.)

On a different piece of paper, stamp as many hearts as you can. Glue the cross-shaped hole over the top of the stamped sheet so that the hearts show through the empty cross.

Talk about the way cross-sections show you what's under the surface of something. What's under the surface of Jesus' cross?

Marshmallow crosses

You will need

Mini marshmallows; cocktail sticks; chocolate dip made by melting Fairtrade chocolate and stirring in single cream to the required consistency (gloopy but not too runny)

Push one marshmallow halfway down one of the cocktail sticks. Push another stick into the marshmallow at right angles to make a cross shape. Then fill up the two cocktail sticks with marshmallows. Dip the marshmallows in the chocolate and eat.

Talk about the fact that Easter is about much more than just chocolate.

String eggs

You will need

Water balloons filled to egg size, then frozen solid; string; PVA glue; water; a shallow dish

Mix up watery PVA glue and put it in a shallow dish. Pull the string through the glue mix, then wrap it around the egg-sized frozen balloon, criss-crossing and overlapping. It's fine to leave gaps. Leave it to dry (it will need to be taken home and dried overnight).

Pop the balloon, let the melted ice drain away, and then ease the balloon out of one of the gaps. You could paint the shape and hang it by a thread.

Talk about the way an Easter egg stands for new life or for the stone in front of Jesus' tomb.

Clean up pennies

You will need

Dirty old coins; white vinegar; salt; glass jar; paper towels; ketchup, Coke and/or lemon juice (optional)

Fill the jar about three-quarters full with vinegar, stir in a teaspoon of salt, drop in your grubby penny and count slowly to ten. (The vinegar reacts with the salt to remove the copper oxide on the coin.) Take the coin out and dry it on the paper towel.

Experiment with different amounts of salt and vinegar. Try it with ketchup or Coke or lemon juice.

Put the money in a pot for charity.

Talk about the way Jesus' death on the cross performed another 'miracle' to start to clean up the bad things in the world.

Prayer station idea

You will need

Sticky notes shaped like arrows; pens; a copy of an icon of the resurrection (search for one on the internet) with these questions written next to it:

- What do you want to say to God about death?
- What do you want to say to God about life after you die?

Write your prayers on the sticky notes and stick them around the picture, close to the part that you think is most important.

Celebration

Story

Take a selection of craft items for each day of the past week and put them in five separate boxes. You could also take photos and display them as a PowerPoint slideshow. You'll also need a rough wooden box for the start of the story and a box of invitations or booklets for the end.

1. A baby was born in a dark place, but his birth brought love, light and laughter to the angels and shepherds who came to see him. The baby had no real home, so they put him in a feeding box instead of a bed. *(Show rough wooden box.)*
2. When the baby grew up, he knew he had come to change the world. So he went round telling people stories to help them know what God is really like and how much God loves them. Stories of… *(Pull items out of the Day 1 box.)*
3. He loved people and always wanted the best for them. He showed them how to break free from what was holding them back. He gathered friends around him—ordinary people, messy people, men and women and children—nobody was left out. *(Pull items out of the Day 2 box.)*
4. He wasn't just a good and generous man; he had amazing powers too. He used these powers to heal people, to show who he was, to bring love, light and laughter back into the world. *(Pull items out of the Day 3 box.)*

5. He walked close to God, his heavenly Father, every day of his life. He showed his friends how to talk and listen to God too. *(Pull items out of the Day 4 box.)*

6. This wonderful man who lived for other people gave up his life so that love and light and laughter could be for everyone for ever. *(Pull crosses out of the Day 5 box.)* But he was so great that even death couldn't hold him down. He came back to life and promised to be with his friends to the end of time. *(Pull resurrection items out of the Day 5 box.)*

7. So this amazing man, with his stories, his love, his power and his closeness to God, is still working miracles in the world today. He invites every one of us to follow him and help bring his love, light and laughter to the people and places that need it. *(Show box of booklets, such as* Messy Readings: The Jesus Story *or invitations to the next event).*

• Song suggestion: 'God behind', Fischy Music

Prayer

Teach actions for the cradle (hold a baby in your arms); the cross (hold arms outstretched); the resurrection (hold arms up). Pray, doing the actions as you speak:

We pray for those at the very beginning of something new (cradle), for those going through hard times (cross) and those at the end of something (resurrection).

We pray for those who need loving (cradle), those who are struggling (cross) and for those who are celebrating (resurrection).

We thank you for all we've discovered and enjoyed at the beginning of this week (cradle), throughout this week (cross) and beyond this week (resurrection).

Messy Grace

May the grace of our Lord Jesus Christ
    (Hold out your hands as if expecting a present)
and the love of God
    (Put your hands on your heart)
and the fellowship of the Holy Spirit
    (Hold hands)
be with us all now and for ever. Amen!
    (Raise hands together on the word 'Amen')

• Song suggestion: 'As we go now' (Fischy Music)

One-day

Messy
Family Fun

Day

*

Overview of the day

This day-long session is a stand-alone session and could be used if you want to do something similar to a full five-day Messy Family Fun Club but can't pull the team together or book a building for that length of time.

The theme for the session is 'Party Animals' and explores some of the different parties that Jesus went to or told stories about. It explores Jesus as someone who lives life to the full, is generous, welcomes everyone and brings communities together to enjoy themselves. Did you know that the word 'party' comes from the Latin word for 'to share'?

The suggested outline is different from the week's programme, as a single day has a different dynamic. It's much more laid-back and less structured, on the grounds that, if a family goes to a Family Fun Day run by their local park, council or community group, it will be in a nice venue with different activities and entertainment going on but not a strict timetable that they have to adhere to.

A one-off day gives the team permission to be more relaxed about 'organising' the families. It simply provides a safe space in which they can enjoy themselves together and explore the day's theme on a level that suits them—more of a drop-in event than an 'arrive at X o'clock and leave at Y o'clock' event. The team doesn't need to have a professional, confident leader or group up front, but there is scope for the day to have more of a focus than if it were just a fête. It also allows space for families to get to know each other around the activities, and leaders should find that they have more time and space to chat to people and start to make friendships than they would at a more tightly organised event.

The range of activities may be inviting for single adults who have come without children. The day will feel more like an event to 'set out your stall'—showcasing your values and attitudes, introducing yourselves as a church and inviting people to other events—than a teaching session.

The programme is simple:

- All day: Messy Church-type activities, including some that take longer than usual to complete
- Ongoing free play corner with sand, water, toys, paint, paper and bubbles
- Lunch: family barbecue
- Afternoon: activities continue alongside a programme of entertainment, with an emphasis on taking part
- Final 'parade' of everything made or practised during the day
- Afternoon tea and cake

Ongoing activities

Party accessories

You will need

Old jeans; needles and thread; sewing machine if you have enough people to supervise; sewing scissors; trimmings (buttons, sequins, patches, stick-on shapes and so on)

Cut the legs off the jeans just above the crotch. Turn the jeans inside out and sew the bottom edges together to make a bag.

From the discarded legs, cut two straps (long or short) and sew them into the bag. Some people may prefer to sew unhemmed strips of fabric on as straps. Other people may prefer to spend time making properly edged straps by making a 'sausage' of fabric, sewn together inside out, then turned the right way out and sewn on to the bag.

Turn the bag the right way out and decorate with trimmings.

Talk about the way you might take this bag to a party, and about the way lots of Jesus' parables ended with parties. Can you think of any? Remember the parables of the lost coin, the lost sheep and the prodigal son?

People parties

> **You will need**
>
> A range of small sellable craft item ideas and the materials to make them—for example, coin purses, marshmallow pingers, party animal jam jars, felt animals, stone creatures (see below)

Make something you can sell in a silent auction during the afternoon, to raise money to help other people. Give the money to a charity that helps others, so that your party will go on beyond the day and beyond your own group of people.

 Tip This could be an opportunity to do activities you've wanted to do at Messy Church but which have never matched the theme.

Coin purses

To make coin purses, see page 26.

Marshmallow pinger

Tie a knot in an uninflated round balloon and cut off about 3 cm from the top so that you're left with the knotted part. Take a yoghurt pot or plastic cup and cut off the bottom so that you're left with an open-ended cylinder. Stretch the balloon over the sturdiest end, with the knot on the outside, to make a 'trampoline'.

When selling the cup, include a little pack of mini marshmallows. To use, place one marshmallow in the cup, resting on the stretched balloon, pull back the knot and fire the marshmallow out.

Party animal jam jars

Beforehand, glue-gun or superglue plastic animals or other shapes to the lids of jam jars. Invite people to come and paint both the jar lid and the animal in the same colour acrylic paint and, when dry, screw the lid back on the jar to make an attractive container. You could put a packet of sweets in the jar to sell it.

Felt animals

Using templates, cut two simple animal or bird shapes roughly 7 cm long, out of felt. Sew the pair of shapes together using blanket stitch. Stuff slightly, sew up completely and attach a thread for hanging.

Stone creatures

Glue googly eyes on to a stone and draw a face on it with a Sharpie pen or permanent marker.

Drink windows

> **You will need**
>
> Black A4 card or sturdy black paper; pencils; rulers; scissors; glue; tissue paper; pictures of cocktails or mocktails

Invite people to cut a glass shape out of the card's centre (fold it in half lengthways and draw half the glass shape along the fold, then cut out the double thickness). Cut or rip pieces of coloured tissue paper and stick them across the empty glass shape to make a multi-layered cocktail picture.

At a wedding that Jesus and his friends attended, there weren't cocktails but there was wine—and even that ran out. What do you think Jesus did? Tell the story from John 2.

Calligraphy party invitations

> **You will need**
>
> Scrap paper; 'nice' paper; calligraphy pens and ink (or felt-tip calligraphy pens); rulers; pencils; erasers; sample alphabets printed out; someone who can teach calligraphy

Practise writing in calligraphy on scrap paper until you feel confident to design an invitation. It can be an invitation of any sort: if you're stuck for an idea, why not design an invitation to the next Messy Church to give to a friend?

Talk about the parable of the great banquet (Luke 14:15–24), and how God's invitation to his party is for everyone.

Wedding costumes

You will need

A range of dressing-up clothes for weddings from different cultures; newspapers; sticky tape; stapler; crêpe paper; coloured paper; scissors; floral wire; air-drying clay; string

Dress up as a bridesmaid, make yourself a wedding hat from newspaper, put together a wedding bouquet or make an oil lamp for a wedding in the old days.

Wedding hat

Spread three sheets of newspaper unevenly over someone's head and wrap sticky tape several times round (as if making the hat fit) to make a base. Fold or scrunch up the edges as tightly or as loosely as you fancy and staple them in place. Decorate with crêpe paper flowers and homemade feathers as desired.

Paper flowers

Draw a spiral on a square of coloured paper and cut it out roughly along the lines. Wind it into itself so that it looks like a rose. Pinch together at the base and tape together. Add floral wire as a stem.

Talk about the parable of the wise and foolish bridesmaids (Matthew 25:1–13) and how they needed oil lamps for weddings in Jesus' day because the celebrations went on late into the night. Weddings take a lot of preparation even today: it's important to be ready for a big event.

Party pompoms

You will need

Lots of coloured tissue paper; gift ribbon; scissors

Place about six sheets of tissue paper on top of each other and concertina-fold them all the way down (across the width) so that you end up with a fat pleat of paper about 4 cm wide. Fold it in half to find the centre spot, make a small notch on either side of the pleat and tie a piece of ribbon around it, fitting it into the notches. Tie the ribbon into a loop as a handle.

At this point you can trim the ends of the paper into a different shape or frill (or petal or point) if you want. Gently ease out the different layers from each other until your pompom is nice and fat. Hold on to the ribbon handle and use during the afternoon entertainment.

Talk about the way God's people have always enjoyed praising God in praise parties using dance and music.

Zacchaeus' chocolate tiffin

You will need

225 g Rich Tea or digestive biscuits; 100 g margarine; 1 tbsp golden syrup; 2 tsp Fairtrade cocoa powder; chocolate icing; paper bun cases; a microwave; bowls; spoons; rolling pins; plastic bags

Make this instant cake. Crush the biscuits by putting them in plastic bags and rolling them with a rolling pin. Melt the margarine and syrup in the microwave (adult supervision needed) and mix with the crushed biscuits and cocoa powder. Press the mixture into bun cases and put chocolate icing on top. Refrigerate if not eating straight away.

Zacchaeus would have needed some very quick recipes to make tea, the day Jesus invited himself round (Luke 19:1–10). He really wasn't expecting such an important guest.

Dangly party decorations

You will need

Clean two-litre plastic bottles; sticky-backed plastic; coloured tape or permanent markers; glue; glitter; scissors; thread or ribbon

Decorate a bottle as brightly as you can with the sticky-backed plastic, tape and pens. Then draw on a spiral all the way round the bottle and cut it out, cutting off the base but leaving the neck part attached at the top. Tie a piece of thread or ribbon on to the neck to hang it up by. Slosh on some glue, roll the bottle in glitter and hang it up to decorate the party.

Talk about how, in the parable of the great banquet, the king made careful preparations for his party so that his guests would have a lovely time. How did he feel when they made excuses not to come?

Pamper corner

You will need

Nail varnish; body butter; massage oils; foot lotion; towels; wipes

There are further ideas in the May–August 2013 issue of *Get Messy!* ('Calming the storm' session).

Have some pampering on offer for anyone who would like it (not only women).

Tell people the story of the party when a woman burst in, poured perfume over Jesus' feet and dried them with her hair. Have you ever been at a party where something surprising happened?

Health and safety

Beware of allergies.

Last Supper miniature kits

You will need

Small tins of the sort used for mints or tobacco; yellow, white and grey air-drying clay (or paint, if you don't have coloured clay); modelling tools; old white hankies; large white sticky labels

Using the clay, make a tiny cup, a plate with bread on it, candlesticks (if desired) and four small cubes to act as table legs. The tin will become a table when balanced on the four 'legs'. Cut a tablecloth out of an old hanky to cover the tin. Make everything small enough to fit inside the tin with the lid shut. Decorate the paper label and stick it over the lid.

Describe Jesus' last and best party, and invite people to retell the story using their own kit.

Easy origami stars

You will need

A4 paper, cut into strips about 2.5 cm wide; string or jars or vases and pea sticks (optional)

Go online and look up 'origami lucky paper stars tutorial'. There are lots of designs, and the one that looks small and puffy and is sometimes called a 'lucky star' is very easy to make. Make lots of them, string them in a line as decorations or fill a jar with them or tape them on top of pea sticks in a vase.

Talk about how much fun it is to have parties and how Jesus loved going to parties.

Decorating cupcakes

You will need

Fairy cakes; icing; decorations; pictures for inspiration (an image search on 'cupcakes fish' will give you more than enough)

Invite people to decorate a fairy cake suitable for a party with lots of fishermen.

Talk about the way Martha and Mary made Jesus and his friends (many of whom were fishermen) welcome in their home. Talk about the friends you like to invite to your home.

Vegetable party animals

You will need

Vegetables; cocktail sticks; googly eyes

Invite people to design the funkiest 'party animal' they can out of vegetables.

Who is the best human 'party animal' you know? Why do you think people were desperate for Jesus to come to their parties?

Musical instruments

Use tubes and bottles, metal lids, boxes, elastic bands and so on to make handheld instruments such as shakers, rain sticks, scrapers, cymbals and plucked 'guitars'.

Alternatively, make larger-scale instruments:

- Hang pots and pans or planks or metal pipes up on ropes and bang them with sticks.
- Make carpet roll-sized rain sticks.
- Make drums out of dustbins.
- Stretch lengths of elastic over wheelie bins to pluck.
- Fill jars and bottles with different amounts of water. Tap the bottles or blow over them.

Talk about whether you prefer quiet or noisy parties.

Party prayer zones

- Cocktail umbrella prayers: Write the name of someone you want to pray for on a block of playdough using a sharp tool. Take a cocktail umbrella, open it up and stick it into the playdough as a sign that God's love is sheltering that person.
- Firework party prayers: Make a backdrop of a night sky with firework rockets soaring across it. On a strip of metallic paper, write or draw a prayer for someone you love. Now make the paper into a star (see the 'Easy origami stars' activity on page 57) and glue it to the backdrop near a firework.
- Beach party prayer stones: Write a 'sorry' prayer on a pebble, using chalk, and drop it into a bowl or pool of water. Come and look for it later, and see how the pebble has been washed clean.
- Pyjama party prayers: Pick a teddy bear and, as you cuddle it, read the prayer on the label around its neck (written in advance by somebody else).
- Tea party prayers: Write 'God' on one side of a small felt heart with a marker pen and 'U' on the other. Carefully remove the tag from a teabag-on-a-string and replace it with the heart, stapling it on. Put the teabag back in its sachet and ask God who he would like you to give it to.

Afternoon entertainment suggestions

Treat the afternoon as an opportunity to stage an activity as if it was in the 'main ring' of a county show. People can either join in with it or enjoy watching it from a safe distance. Here are some suggestions, but a lot will rely on your local talent.

- Puppets: Put on a puppet show, followed by a workshop where people can come and learn how to use a puppet and join in a song, especially if you have some indestructible sock puppets or glove puppets that you'd be happy for less careful people to use.
- Family treasure hunt: Arrange a scavenger hunt with 20 things to collect, or send people round your building to discover some of the interesting parts of it for themselves.
- Family film: *VeggieTales*, *Friends and Heroes* and *The Miracle Maker* are all gentle introductions to Bible stories, suitable for all ages.
- Sports: Organise games to enthral the livelier participants.

- Learn a dance: Invite someone to teach some basic street dance moves.
- Learn a song: Use the musical instruments made at the activity table.
- Costume parade: Set up a catwalk and model the hats and flowers made in the wedding activity above.
- Circus skills: Try juggling, diabolo, plate spinning, unicycling and so on.
- Messy challenges: Wheel in youth leaders or look up 'messy games for youth groups' on the internet. There are amazing quantities of really messy games involving jelly, porridge, sponges, baked beans or even just water. Choose those that you feel only faintly nervous about. Have macs, clean-up facilities and spare dry clothes available.
- Big scribble art challenge: On very large sheets of paper, draw very large scribbles. The challenge is for each team to turn their scribble into a picture, using paints or pens, in three minutes. The winner is the best picture.
- Trafalgar triangle: This is a two-minute talent show or soapbox. In Trafalgar Square, the Fourth Plinth is left empty for anyone to book time on it and do whatever they like from the top of it (within reason). Offer the opportunity to have two minutes on your own plinth. Make sure rent-a-crowd is ready to applaud wildly at the end of each two-minute offering.
- Silent auction of crafts for local charity: Set out all the items you have made for sale in the activity above, with a sheet of wide-spaced lined paper taped next to each one and lots of pens available. Make it clear that the auction is to raise money for a good cause. Explain to everyone that they have 20 minutes (or less if there isn't much to sell) to go round, writing on the paper the price they will pay for the item and their name. They will obviously need to put down a higher bid than the highest one already on the paper. Give a ten- and five-minute warning and, at the end, have your minions guard the papers jealously to prevent unscrupulous people from adding a bid after the deadline.

Stories of other Messy Church-related holiday clubs

Story 1: PACT Holiday Club

Helen Mason, Emma Dean and team run a Messy Church holiday club in Petersfield, Hampshire. The Petersfield Area Churches Together (PACT) team had held very successful children-only holiday clubs for many years, but in 2011 they decided to build on the success of the joint Messy Church by changing to a family-based holiday club in its place.

I asked if the families objected to staying with the children, having got used to dropping their children off over the years.

The answer is both yes and no. Some parents need a holiday club scheme that is a 'drop and go', while others want to be involved with the children. One mum said that, as the parent of a single child, without an opportunity like this it would be possible for her daughter to spend the whole holiday without meeting another child. The team try to 'attach' two families together so that they share responsibility, one working parent bringing the children of both families on one day and the other bringing them all on the next day. The activity style is what so many parents want—enough space to give children freedom but having the parents near enough to stop any mischief.

Helen and Emma continue:

PACT Holiday Club was held at the Petersfield School from Monday 30 July to Friday 3 August with the theme 'Church, God's Brilliant Idea'. Local members of the clergy led the morning talks, with Lyndsey Gilbey from Fiddlesticks and her team leading the singing (**www. fiddlesticksmusic.co.uk**).

On the Wednesday, part of the focus was on loving our communities, and the children were extremely generous in their offerings to the Petersfield Foodbank.

The holiday club is divided into two sections—under-8s and Juniors—and the Juniors choose one activity to focus on for the week, which they then present to the under-8s and families on the Friday. Over 50 Junior children attended during the week.

The under-8s section is prepared in a Messy Church style, with ten activities each day and also playball, Fiddlesticks and hands-on science sessions. Each day there are plenty of opportunities for the children to do a huge variety of craft activities as well as attending Fiddlesticks sessions with Lyndsey and playball sessions led by Kerrie

Elsom and her team. Some of the older children were given the chance to do some science with local scientist Dr Phil Jupp.

We had 81 families attend the Messy Church sessions during the week, with an average of 95 children attending each day. In total we had 101 families signed up for the PACT Holiday Club divided across the age groups, and over 80 adults attending daily. The Holiday Club has been run in many different ways over the years. When we made the changes to it three years ago, we knew that parents wanted more involvement with the summer activities that their children attended, but we hadn't appreciated at the time just how bereft some parents feel during the six-week summer holiday. Three years ago, there wasn't much choice for children during the summer holidays in Petersfield. We're now involved in a highly competitive market for childcare, but we offer a rare style of activity group as we include the parents and only run for the mornings. For us, it is about meeting the parents' needs as much as it is about the children having fun.

PACT Holiday Club is supported by volunteers from the local churches, and this year we had support from some Guides as well. Without this support the event couldn't have run.

Story 2: Messy weekend away

Alison Thurlow, from near Bristol, writes about an exciting Messy weekend away.

In the summer of 2012, as we approached the end of our third year of running Messy Church at St Nicholas Church in Yate, I started dreaming about a Messy Church weekend away in the summer of 2013. I talked to a few people about my idea; all seemed keen, but where was I to go from there? I needed to think of a venue, enthuse a few more people, start publicising the event…

• September 2012: Five of us visited 'Great Wood', the Scripture Union site in the Quantocks, and fell in love with the place; the group included my chief cook, who thought the kitchen was fab—phew! We had some good-quality flyers designed as soon as we got home and budgeted for 50 people. We chose a date when

GCSEs and A Levels would be finished and when university students would be home for the summer.

- October 2012: We distributed flyers at Messy Church asking for a fairly modest deposit by the end of November. There was an air of excitement and anticipation about the place as we started talking about this new venture.
- November 2012: 77 people applied to come to Great Wood. We established a 'bank' system so that people could pay in small instalments over the next eight months.
- January 2013: There was much slightly anxious correspondence with the amazingly helpful and gracious Great Wood staff, who answered my myriad questions.
- February 2013: I met with the cook to plan the menus and checked that we had some qualified first-aiders coming.
- April 2013: We booked a lifeguard so that we could use the swimming pool. People were reminded that the balance of payment would be due in the next month.
- May 2013: All money having been paid in, informal chats about the programme took place. Chalets were allocated and a letter sent to everyone coming, giving more details about the weekend. Rotas were drawn up and kitchen and washing-up helpers were decided. The teenagers agreed to take on all the washing-up between them.
- Early June 2013: We did an online supermarket order to have most of the food delivered to the site. The team met to finalise plans for crafts, games and other activities.

On 28 June 2013, 77 of us, aged between 2 and 70, set off for Great Wood in the Quantocks. There was huge excitement all around, as well as some degree of trepidation on my part: how would all these people, who had only ever spent two hours together once a month on a Saturday afternoon, really get on when they spent 48 hours in very close proximity?

I need not have worried: we all had the most fantastic weekend. The weather was wonderful, the venue was beautiful and the wooden cabins that we slept in were much better than anticipated. The food was fabulous, many new friendships were formed and the teenagers were exemplary, both in terms of all the work they did and also in the way they looked after some of the younger children, giving parents a much-needed rest. The balance of activity and free time seemed about right. The Sunday morning celebration was both great fun and very meaningful, and it felt as though Messy Church had moved to a new level in the quality of relationships between people.

Would I do it again? Well, yes—next year, actually!

Story 3: Messy Boomerang

Claire Johnson from Locks Heath near Southampton writes:

For eight years Locks Heath Free Church has been running an annual week-long summer holiday club called Boomerang, using two local primary schools as well as the church building. At its height it has reached 600 children aged 0–11 years.

This year (our ninth) we faced the challenge that the schools were no longer available. For Boomerang to happen at the church alone, we needed to restructure it, so we asked ourselves which elements we were not prepared to lose. One thing that we felt was essential to maintain was the facility for parents to attend with the under-5s.

We had started Messy Church on a Sunday afternoon in October 2012 and were already seeing God use it as a bridge between our midweek community families and Sunday church. We therefore decided to combine Boomerang and Messy Church and run 'Messy Boomerang', inviting parents to attend with their children of all ages. There was some opposition, and some families chose not to come because they had to come with their children, but we still felt it was the right step to take.

Each morning's programme was as follows:

9.15 am	Team arrives for prayer and briefing, followed by refreshments.
10.00 am	Registration (doors open 9.50)
10.10–10.30 am	Under-5s Messy celebration (nursery rhymes; theme intro, using puppets; song; Bible story; memory verse song; creative prayer; theme song)
10.10–10.30 am	School Years 5 and 6: Session 1 (no parents allowed)
10.00–11.30 am	Activities open: seven craft activities, three challenges, big games and creative prayer tent, based on daily themes
11.30–12 noon	Over-5s Messy celebration (warm-up, song, theme intro quiz, Bible story/application, game, theme song)
11.30–12 noon	School Years 5 and 6: Session 2 (no parents allowed)
12.00 noon	Home time

We had an under-5s marquee with free play, themed play, playdough, face painting, bouncy castle and soft play; also a café serving free drinks, biscuits and amazing home-made cakes for a minimal charge. This was where many significant relationships were built, as well as over the activities.

A minimum of two team members were involved in each activity so that they could engage in conversations rather than just explaining what to do.

We also ran a crèche for under-2s. This was used by the team, and parents with older children also appreciated having time to focus on them.

The week was a huge success—way beyond our expectations. We welcomed 216 children and about 150 adults. It was a joy to see the parents move from watching on the sidelines, getting more and more involved in the activities and celebrations as the week progressed. A highlight of the week was 'Water Day', when many of the activities involved getting very wet.

We finished the week with a family picnic straight after the final session. I have never had as many people coming up to say 'thank you for a fantastic week' as at the end of Messy Boomerang.

Boomerang has always resulted in new children joining our midweek activities, but never at the level of this year. At our September Messy Church, four new families came as a direct result of Boomerang, including one family in which the mum had done Boomerang with the two kids but it was the dad's first time in the church. By the end of the song he was joining in the actions too. We are looking forward to watching relationships deepen as the year unfolds and we expect to see great things.

Will we return to Boomerang as it was? No... Messy Boomerang is here to stay!

Story 4: Messy Church summer programme

Becky Wapshot from Dedridge Baptist Church, West Lothian, writes:

Over the last couple of years we have run holiday time family mornings, open to anyone, with a mixture of crafts, games, sports, food, story and worship. Previously we only ran them once in each holiday period—Easter, summer, October, Christmas, February and so on. They were generally very well attended by the community, with a wide range of families and a similarly wide range in terms of where people were on their faith journeys.

Earlier this year we evaluated the strengths and weaknesses of our family mornings. We realised that many of their strengths were similar to Messy Church. Having spent more time finding out about Messy Church, we were really keen to adapt and improve our existing work by using the Messy Church values and principles.

We decided that we could do five separate Messy Church mornings on holiday weekdays over the year and a more intense block of six Messy Church sessions over the summer holidays.

We started at the deep end, in the summer, and ran a two-hour programme every Wednesday through the holidays. The overall theme was God the creator, and each week looked at a different aspect, starting with the creation story and ending with a focus on Psalm 8. We wanted to show that even though God created all the amazing things we had looked at over the summer, he made us really special too, and gave us the most important job of looking after his world.

Each morning started with tea, coffee and juice and a welcome activity, then gathering together for welcome and introduction to the theme/story, followed by an hour of activity options including challenges, crafts, games, messy play and prayer stations. Generally there were about 10 to 15 stations. We were short of helpers, as it was the summer holiday, so not every station had its own helper each week, but it was encouraging to see some of the adults just joining in and helping other families. After the activity hour, we went into another room for juice and snacks, and, while everyone was tucking in, we had a story time and prayer activity.

Over the summer, more than 200 people came, averaging 76 people per week. These numbers were much greater than we had expected and every week there were new people. Not very many came every week, but we had expected that, as it was summer holiday time. People came from right across town: some had received flyers through the local school, some had heard about it through health or council information and others through word of mouth and social media.

It was a fantastic summer. God really blessed Messy Church here and it was so exciting to be part of it. We asked for feedback at the end of the summer and are considering whether we need to offer more sessions during the year. Some of the biggest encouragements for us were meeting families with whom we've have had no previous contact, having new people ask to be involved and help out, the questions asked by children and adults alike, and the huge range of people who came along and who make up the Messy Church team. It touched so many lives in our community, and even people who didn't come along were telling me that they'd been given a craft item by their grandchild and had heard why they had made it.

One of the learning points was that we need a bigger team, and we're hoping that some of the families who became helpers over the summer will want to stay on the team and be part of Messy Church in the long term. We also only provided snacks over the summer, because of the high and fluctuating numbers, but we felt that we missed out on a good chance to chat by not sharing food around a table.

The feedback from the families was really encouraging. Many came because it was something free to do, but what they got out of it was so very much more, and many of them were keen to share just what the summer at Messy Church had meant to them. Some of our families who come to church on a Sunday were also able to come along, and for them it gave valuable time and space in which they could worship and share faith together as a family and with other families in the community.

Story 5: Mestival!

Chris Alexander writes:

We held our Messy Church 'Mestival' on the August Bank Holiday weekend, from Sunday at 3.00 pm till Monday at about the same time. We camped out in the school field at Waltham on the Wolds Primary School, and the school generously allowed us access to the loos, as well as water and electricity to power our hot water urn. Also, the preschool kindly let us use their veranda and tricycles.

We were blessed with 26 adults and 21 children, including two babies, and the weather was very pleasant, dry and warm. We had a few games of rounders, played with bubbles, explored the wood, had a barbecue in the evening, and did some art and a bit of pond-dipping as well as generally relaxing and enjoying the sun. We also held a short service on the Sunday evening. Highlights included toasting marshmallows over a log fire and having bacon sandwiches for breakfast.

Story 6: Messy Church Family Funday

Syl Hunt, Regional Coordinator in Cumbria, writes:

After much prayer, preparation and planning, and a week of rain, Wednesday 14 August dawned bright and sunny. We sprang into action to:

- display Messy Church, 'Shackles Off' and 'Hope in Seascale' banners on the sea front
- fasten balloons and bunting along the sea front

- erect a gazebo for face painting, cake decorating and jenga jelly (playing jenga on a bowl of jelly)
- blow up the paddling pool and fill it with water for 'Hook a duck'
- set up the tin can alley
- set up large outdoor games—snakes and ladders, ludo, Twister and beat-the-bleep
- mow the grass for a crazy golf course and set it up
- set up tables for crafts, £10 buried treasure in a sand tray, and sweets in a jar

All the above activities were on offer all day. Every hour, for approximately 15 minutes we had Primary Puppets from Northern Inter-Schools Christian Union telling about the love of Jesus in song. In between, Albert and his merry band entertained us with their music. Ruth, who was in the juggling society at Portsmouth University, did a juggling challenge (something we had enjoyed when we juggled with fruit in a previous Messy Church session, as we talked about the fruit of the Spirit).

A couple from church ran some kite-flying lessons on the beach, using amazing kites from all over the world. People also brought their own and were awarded kite-flying certificates. During the day there was a seashore treasure hunt, as well as sandcastle building competitions, parachute games and a tug of war.

One of the most exciting events was the donkey race. My original thought was that we could have had real donkeys on the beach, but they would have cost us £200, and then people would have been charged for the rides, thus preventing us from offering everything free of charge. Praise the Lord for *Get Messy!* magazine, which came just at the right time, offering advice on donkey making in its Christmas session. People thought they were a great idea and loved racing them on the beach.

There were lots of blessings from the day:

- Being in the community
- Meeting new people and receiving enquiries about Messy Church
- Seeing everyone's amazement at being offered the activities
- The beautiful weather
- The little boy who wanted to come back the next day
- The Parish Council waiving the donation for the electricity used, as it was a community event
- The willingness of businesses to donate sweets and ice cream for prizes, and the positive effect the day had on their businesses
- Only one first-aid treatment needed—for my daughter Martha, who was stung by a wasp
- A good report in the *Whitehaven News* and a letter of thanks the week after

- One grandad who thought it was great, especially as his granddaughters went straight to sleep that night
- The person who was very honest and returned the 'treasure in the sand tray' prize as it was pushed through the wrong letterbox
- The sweets in a jar won by a Messy Church family— the children were so excited.

People really appreciated the day, and it is definitely worth doing it again next year. Even now, an idea is brewing in my head for a 'Mega Messy Christmas'.

*

Epilogue

Rona Stuart-Bourne, curate at St Peter's, Portsmouth, wrote two months after the Messy Family Fun Club:

And a month after that:

We are so delighted with the ripples of enthusiasm which still rebound around Somers Town. We had a baptism recently and, as Alex was introducing the service, I kept spotting mums from the week and mouthing 'hello' to them. They were all beaming, and afterwards a few said they felt comfortable coming into the church! Wasn't that lovely?

I'm not sure if Alex or Alan have told you that we are doing our next Messy Church today. I thought I'd just feed back to you, having read your blog about Messy Family Fun. We had 40 booked, and 90 came! So many of our original families from that week came, with others who were encouraged in by the things they had heard about it. One of the things a few people said was that they hadn't known many people in Somers Town before, but having met them at our Messy Family Fun they were now friends, and were thrilled to be together again.

There were obvious issues: the background noise caused by the adults getting on so well meant that the telling of the story was quite tough! Also, we could really have used that top bloke Jesus when we had to stretch 40 meals into 90. We managed, though.

Powerful, profound conversations happened, and it was such a privilege to be part of them.

Downloadable appendices

This section gives examples of forms, planning aids and publicity for your Messy Family Fun Club, as follows:

These pages are available as Word documents that can be customised. They are also available as PDF downloads: please go to www.messychurch.org.uk/9780857463050/.

Messy Family Fun Club: Team recruitment

Date: _____

Place: _____

The plan: We are going to hold an exciting and groundbreaking event: a **Messy Church Family Fun Club**! Think Holiday Club but for the whole family, where families can come and enjoy exploring faith and fun together for a whole week of the holiday.

The vision: To run a holiday club-type programme of crafts, activities, a meal, story, games and skills for whole families for five days. It will be **worship, mission, outreach, social action, community**, the church doing what it does best—throwing its doors open to everyone who wants to meet God, meeting them with fun, laughter and learning through enjoyment, and helping each other encounter the living Lord Jesus. It will be one part of the wider picture of our strategy for families. All children (under 18) need to be accompanied by an adult (18+).

How will it work?

The Messy Family Fun Club will run from 10.00 am to 1.00 pm each day. The programme will be along these lines:

- 10.00 start
- Welcome
- Short gathering celebration
- Ten fun activities to explore the biblical theme (40 minutes)
- Coffee break
- Extreme family skills (30 minutes)
- Short closing celebration
- 12.00 lunch

We need you!

Can you bring your gifts and skills to serve others in this exciting venture? We need people to pray for us... team members to lead craft activities and explain the gospel through them... team members to share a life skill (as exciting as possible, from cooking, sport, wiring a plug, taking apart an engine, drama, dance and technology to tying knots, sawing wood and bike maintenance). We need a cooks' team, a clear-up team to come in afterwards, and others.

If you're interested in helping with any aspect of this project (ideally for the whole week but it's OK if you can only offer one day) please contact or sign up on the sheet in the church.

 Reproduced with permission from *Messy Family Fun* by Lucy Moore (Messy Church, 2015) www.messychurch.org.uk

Messy Family Fun Club: Team sign-up sheet

Please fill in your details here

Name	Email	Mobile	Days available	Will have my own children with me (Yes/No)	'Extreme skill' I could lead	Preferred involvement (if not general team member) e.g. clear-up team, cooks' team, prayer team

The information supplied on this form will be retained by our church on a database and will be used only for the administration of the Messy Family Fun Club. It will not be disclosed to any third parties.

Messy Family Fun Club: Helpers under 18

Activity: helping on the team at the Messy Family Fun Club

Leader of holiday club: _____

Contact number: _____

Young person's details

Name: _____

Address: _____

Mobile: _____

Any medical, dietary or special needs: _____

Family doctor's name, address and phone number: _____

_____

☐ I give consent for my child to take part in this event.

☐ I consent to my child being transported in a team member's car if required.

☐ I agree to photographs/film of activities including my child to be used within the church community and for possible publication, including in newspapers and books and on the internet. I understand that this promotion might be made online, printed, as in newsletters or brochures, or extended to any other type of media, as in reports and articles, videos and DVDs and so on about Messy Church. I also understand that neither further notice on the part of the church nor any further permission is required to use such pictures/film for the above promotional purposes.

☐ I am aware that the church will always ensure:

• that the pictures and video used are respectful in their nature and appropriate/relevant to the activity promoted.
• that no link can be made between the image of my child and his/her full name (only first name will be used), address, email and so on, in order to avoid personal information being displayed or accessed publicly.

☐ I agree to any emergency medical treatment to be given as considered necessary by the medical authorities if I cannot be contacted.

Signed (parent/carer): _____ Date _____

Parent's/carer's name: _____

Address (if different from above): _____

Emergency phone number: _____ Alternative emergency number: _____

The information supplied on this form will be retained by our church on a database and will be used only for the administration of the Messy Family Fun Club. It will not be disclosed to any third parties.

 Reproduced with permission from *Messy Family Fun* by Lucy Moore (Messy Church, 2015) www.messychurch.org.uk

Messy Family Fun Club: Information for families

[Dates]

Join us at _____ for

Messy Family Fun Club!

10.00 am–1.00 pm including lunch

A holiday club for the whole family

Activities for everyone—adults, teenagers and children. Do some art and craft, music and sport; learn new skills together, meet some fantastic visitors from the city with unexpected treats, get in touch with God, make new friends and enjoy a hot meal.

This is a family event: children (under 18) must be accompanied by an adult (18+) and adults remain responsible for their children throughout. Maximum **four** children per adult.

Cost: £ _____ per family per day including meal, drinks and all materials and activities

- 10.00: Welcome chill time
- 10.10: Short get-together
- 10.20: Fun activities with a Bible theme—craft, games, space, prayer, mess—do as many as you like
- 11.00: Coffee break
- 11.10: Extreme family skills—choose whichever you like
- 11.45: Short celebration
- 12.00: Hot lunch

Places are limited, so it's advisable to book in good time.

Please fill in the booking form and send with the full payment to: _____

_____

Messy Family Fun Club: Booking form

Please complete one form per family

Name _____

Address _____

Email _____

Mobile _____

I would like to book places for the following adult(s) and children/teenagers.

Names of adults

1 _____

2 _____

3 _____

4 _____

Full names and ages of children/teenagers

1 _____

2 _____

3 _____

4 _____

Please list any dietary requirements or food allergies you would like us to be aware of:

_____

Are there any medical conditions or special needs we should be aware of?

_____

The cost per family per day is £ _____   Please make cheques payable to _____

I enclose the full cost for the week of £ _____

Messy Family Fun Club: Photography and film consent

I, _____ (full name of parent /carer)

grant permission to take pictures of/film my child/children:

_____ (child's full name)

_____ (child's full name)

_____ (child's full name)

_____ (child's full name)

for the purpose of publications and promotions.

I understand that this promotion might be made online, printed (as in newsletters, books or brochures) or extended to any other type of media, as in reports and articles, videos, DVDs and so on about Messy Church.

I also understand that neither further notice on the part of the church, nor any further permission, is required to use such pictures/film, for the above promotional purposes.

I am aware that the church will always ensure:

- that the pictures and video used are respectful in their nature and appropriate/relevant to the activity promoted.
- that no link can be made between the image of my child and his/her full name (only first name will be used), address, email, etc. in order to avoid personal information being displayed or accessed publicly.

Date: _____

Signature: _____

The information supplied on this form will be retained by our church on a database and will be used only for the administration of the Messy Family Fun Club. It will not be disclosed to any third parties.

Messy Family Fun Club: Risk assessment

Hazard	Risk	Risk to whom	Likelihood (low/ medium/ high)	Severity (1 to 6)	Existing control measures	Residual risk (1 to 6)	Risk acceptable? (Yes or state action when and by whom)
Child protection	Abuse by team members	Children	L	6	Team members to have DBS checks. All team members to have basic safeguarding good practice outlined verbally.	1	Yes
Child protection	Abuse by visiting helpers who only attend for occasional sessions	Children	L	6	Team members and adults in attendance to supervise children and ensure only very limited exposure of children to the visitors.	1	Yes
Losing children	Children leaving the building on their own	Children	M	5	Team alert to dangers. All possible doors locked (fire escapes needed). Members reminded daily that children are parents' responsibility. All made aware daily of rules about staying in the building.	2	Yes
Fire	Fire	All	L	6	Fire procedures outlined to all on a daily basis	1	Yes

 Reproduced with permission from *Messy Family Fun* by Lucy Moore (Messy Church, 2015) www.messychurch.org.uk

Hazard	Risk	Risk to whom	Likelihood (low/ medium/ high)	Severity (1 to 6)	Existing control measures	Residual risk (1 to 6)	Risk acceptable? (Yes or state action when and by whom)
Injury	From running, from activities (cuts, swallowing, choking, allergies)	All	M	3	Each team member to be aware of risks involved in individual activities. All families to be made aware verbally at a 'risky' activity. Rule of no running except if permission given for sport activity. First aider and kit appointed. Accidents recorded.	1	Yes

Messy Family Fun Club: Safeguarding Policy Statement

1 The only unaccompanied children at the Messy Family Fun Club will be team members under the age of 18 who will complete permission forms beforehand.

2 All other children will be accompanied by an adult or adults and will remain the responsibility of these adults for the duration of the Messy Family Fun Club.

3 All team members will be briefed beforehand on appropriate behaviour with the adults and children attending and on safety issues.

4 All helpers above the age of 16 who are helping for the majority of the week will have appropriate DBS clearance as recommended by the denomination. The risks pertaining to the visiting activity leaders who only attend occasional sessions have been weighed and the core team has decided that it is not necessary for them to have DBS checks carried out.

5 Open doors: the team will be alert to the dangers of children going outside. Parents are responsible for their own children and will be reminded of this every day. The whole Messy Family Fun Club will be reminded daily of the basic rules: stay where your parent can see you; stay in the building unless you have told your parent; don't go anywhere without a grown-up.

6 Fire: a fire safety officer will be appointed and all members will be made aware of the procedure for safe evacuation if there should be a fire.

7 Injury: a first aider will be appointed and a full first aid kit will be to hand. Activity helpers will make families aware of any risks involved—for example, small items to swallow, allergies, sharp blades. Running will be prohibited except for the sport activity. Accidents will be recorded.

Do

- Sign in at start of session and out at the end. Let _____ know if you need to leave before the end.
- Take the initiative.
- If you have any concerns of any sort, report in confidence to _____ . If you have concerns about _____ , report to _____ .
- If children are behaving inappropriately, speak to their parent in the first instance unless the behaviour is immediately dangerous.
- Work in an open environment with no secrets.
- Treat all with respect.
- Put others' welfare first.
- Be positive, encouraging and enthusiastic.
- Be a great role model.

Don't

- Take photos with people in them.
- Spend any time alone with anyone away from others.
- Use mobile phones.
- Engage in rough/inappropriate horseplay.
- Mutter / grumble / complain / gossip about any concerns, and don't listen to grumbles, mutters or gossip; build each other up instead.
- Touch inappropriately.
- Share details of your phone number, personal Facebook page or similar or invite anyone to your home without checking with the leader.
- Allow anyone to use inappropriate language unchallenged.
- Share the toilet with anyone.
- Do anything for anyone that they can do for themselves.

Timings

- 8.30–9.15: Team arrive and prepare
- 9.15: Team prayer
- 10.00: Welcome chill time with filler activity
- 10.10: Short get-together
- 10.20: Fun activities with Bible theme
- 11.00: Coffee break
- 11.10: Extreme family skills
- 11.45: Short celebration
- 12.00: Lunch

Information for team members

Leader's mobile number: _____

Fire safety officer: _____

First aider: _____

Daily planning sheet

Day _____

Job	Name(s)
Prayer meeting leader	
Welcome team	
Leader of welcome activity	
Opening gathering leaders	

Activity	Led by
1	
2	
3	
4	
5	
6	
7	
8	
9	
10	

Coffee team

Extreme family skills	Led by
1	
2	
3	
4	
5	

Celebration team

Lunch team

Clear-up team

Daily activity planner

Day 1 Activity	Notes	Who	Preparation	Health and Safety
Donkey balloon racing				Tripping hazard
Pig biscuits/Pigs' dinner				Hygiene; allergies
Sheep badges				Sharp pins
Coin purse				
Mini mosaics				Swallowing hazard
Story bags				
Banqueting table mats				Laminator: heat/tripping
Giant tree				
Building on jelly				Hygiene; don't eat jelly
Shaving foam marbling				
Prayer station				

Day 2 Activity	Notes	Who	Preparation	Health and Safety
Fishing crew				
Money box				
'Give her something to eat' butty				Hygiene; allergies
Secret messages				
Volcano				Use goggles
Loo-roll wrapping				
River Jordan				
Soap making				Trip/scalding hazards
T-shirt decorating				Trip/dry heat hazards
No easy ride				
Prayer station				

Day 3 Activity	Notes	Who	Preparation	Health and Safety
Walk on the waves challenge				
Blindfold painting				
Five thousand people				
Wine-glass painting				
Spaghetti nets/Bottle fish				Water hazard
Storms in bottles				Drinking hazard
Family scrapbooking				
Party cocktails				
House model				Falling boxes
Pustulous boils				Allergies
Prayer station				

Day 4 Activity	Notes	Who	Preparation	Health and Safety
String telephones				
Prayer cube				
Early in the morning clockwork				
Prayer cupboards				
Prayer treasure hunt				
Teaspoons				
Prayer ice game				
Doodle prayers				
Hat for a Pharisee				
Bubble snakes				Inhalation hazard
Prayer station				

Day 5 Activity	Notes	Who	Preparation	Health and Safety
Story egg box				
Dramatic cross				
Phone photos of crosses				
Adventure challenge				
Shadow puppets				
Exploding tomb sculpture				
Cross section				
Marshmallow crosses				
String eggs				
Clean up pennies				
Prayer station				

There is also a PowerPoint slideshow master for use with your team:
see www.messychurch.org.uk/9780857463050/

3, 2, 1
1, 2, 3
Thank you, God,
For feeding me!

Spectacles template

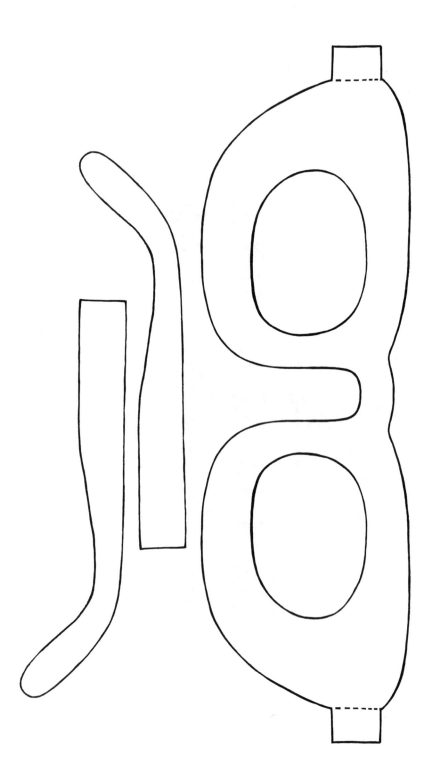

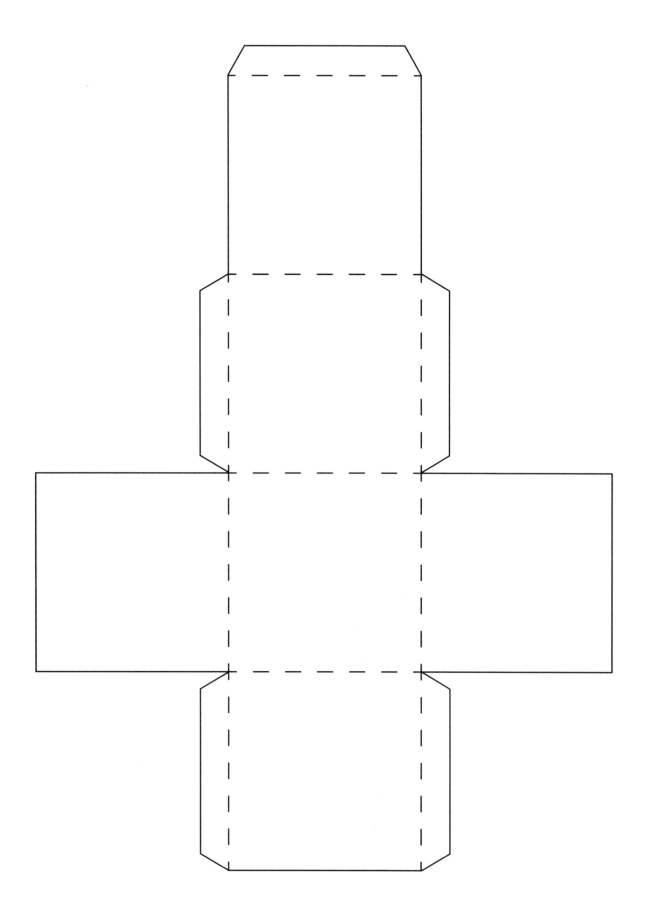

Donkey balloon racing

Make a donkey from a balloon and race it.

Jesus told a story about a man who helped a stranger on to his own donkey when nobody else would help him.

Does anything stop you helping other people?

Pig biscuits

Put a pig in a pen on your biscuit.

Jesus told a story about a boy who made such bad choices that he ended up in the worst place ever, mucking out pigs! But his father loved him so much that he welcomed him back.

How many times do you think God welcomes us back when we make bad choices?

Coin purse

Make a coin purse from recycled materials.

Jesus told a story about a woman who lost one coin.

Was she bothered? Why do you think Jesus told this story?

Sheep badges

Choose from two different designs to make a sheep badge.

Jesus told a story about a man who cared about his sheep so much that he went to look for it when it got lost.

Have you ever felt lost? Did anyone come looking for you? How did that feel?

Mini mosaics

Make a treasure-filled mosaic of your own on the tile. You can take it home or leave it here to make a display and take it home at the end of the week.

Listen to Jesus' story of the man who found buried treasure.

What do you think the story means?

Story bags

Decorate a bag to fill with things you want to take home.

What will you take home that's invisible and can't be put in the bag?

Banqueting table mats

Decorate your own table mat to take home. You can use it to help you say 'thank you' to God for your meals.

Listen to Jesus' story about a great feast.

What do you like best in the story?

Giant tree

Make the biggest tree of all and make a bird to take home.

Jesus told a funny story about a man who planted a seed that grew and grew and grew until it was the biggest tree of all and the birds came and nested in its branches.

What on earth did he mean?

Building on jelly

How high can you build on jelly?

Does your building stay up when you wobble the jelly?

Jesus told a story about two builders who chose to build on different bases (but not jelly).

Shaving foam marbling

Make a mess, then make something beautiful out of it.

In Jesus' story, one man was in a mess and forgiveness helped him out of the mess. But then what did he do to his friend…?

Prayer stations

Use the items below to say some quiet prayers to God, then find out from the other activities which stories today are about sheep, coins and seeds.

Sheep: Put the sheep back in the pen with the others. Thank God for loving you as much as a shepherd loves his sheep.

Chocolate coins: Take one chocolate coin and ask God to help you to find real treasure in your life.

Seeds: Feel how tiny the mustard seeds are and think what they might turn into. Ask God to take your life and turn it into something unimaginably wonderful for him.

Fishing crew

Make a member of the crew to go in the fishing boat with Jesus!

Jesus calls all sorts of messy people to be his friends: he loves you just as you are.

Some of the first people he called were fishermen, and he said to them, 'Follow me and I will make you into fishers of people!'

Money box

Make a money box by glueing on collage scraps to decorate a tin.

Zacchaeus was in love with money until Jesus called him and he saw what was even more important. What did he do with his money then?

What will you spend your money on? How happy are you to share with others who need it even more?

'Give her something to eat' butty

Make the perfect sandwich with a variety of breads and fillings to choose from.

Jesus brought a girl back from the dead and told her parents to give her something to eat.

Secret messages

Write a secret message for someone to discover.

Nicodemus wanted to follow Jesus, but started by doing it secretly.

Why do you think he did this?

Volcano

Make a volcano erupt!

Martha wanted to follow Jesus but she exploded with anger at her sister for not helping with the work. She had to learn to stop and sit and listen to Jesus.

When do you make time to stop and sit and listen to Jesus?

Loo roll wrapping

Mummify someone from your family! You could compete with another family for the best-wrapped mummy.

Jesus was deeply sad when his friend Lazarus died, and he cares when we are sad.

What makes you sad?

River Jordan

Lie down in the river and get someone from your family to draw round you. Then colour in the 'you' in the River Jordan.

John the Baptist told everyone that they needed to get ready for Jesus by being baptised in the river.

Have you seen where people are still baptised, perhaps in this building?

Soap making

Make some soap to take home.

Lots of people felt clean again after Jesus had helped them to get rid of their past lives and start again—people with diseases that he healed, or people who had done terrible things and needed forgiveness.

What would you like Jesus to wash away for you so that you can start again?

T-shirt decorating

Decorate a T-shirt so that it shows something about what you're enjoying this week.

Some people who lived before Jesus looked forward to his coming and wrote about him before he was even on earth. They were called prophets. They acted like signposts, pointing people to Jesus.

When people see your T-shirt, they might ask you where you made it, and you can point them to Jesus and the Messy Family Fun Club.

No easy ride

Make a model jeep to ride on tough adventures.

Jesus never promised anyone it would be easy to follow him. In fact, he said it would be a rough ride!

Why do you think people still follow Jesus, even when it's hard?

Prayer stations

1) Place a paper person on the road, close to or far from the cross, to show how near you feel to Jesus at the moment. Ask Jesus to help you take a step nearer to him this week.

2) Write or draw a friend's name or picture on a tiny sticky note. Do this for as many friends as you like. Write one for yourself too. Pin the notes to the board.
    Pray for your friends by tying one end of the thread to the cross, and winding it slowly round each friend's pin in turn, asking Jesus to bless that friend as you do so.

3) 'The sweet smell of incense can make you feel good, but true friendship is better still' (Proverbs 27:9).
    Come and smell the perfumes. Talk about how it makes you feel and which smells make you feel relaxed and refreshed. Talk about the words from Proverbs and which of your friends make you happy.
    Take away a swab doused in the perfume you prefer. When you sniff it, thank God for those friends, and thank God for Jesus, who wants to be our friend.

Walk on the waves challenge

Can you walk on our 'waves?'

Jesus was so powerful that he could even walk across a stormy sea to his friends.

Is there anything he can't do?

Blindfold painting

Can you paint a picture while blindfolded?

Jesus had so much power that he even made people whose eyes didn't work see again.

What is the most beautiful thing you can see around you at this moment?

Five thousand people

We need 5000 men (plus women and children) who all had enough to eat when Jesus fed them with just five rolls and two fish!

Help to print them and keep a tally.

What seems impossible to us is possible for God. He can do *anything!*

Wine-glass painting

Paint a beautiful wine glass that Jesus might have used at a wedding when the wine ran out.

He turned water into the best wine ever!

What parts of your life would you like Jesus to transform, just as he changed the water into wine?

Spaghetti nets

Drag spaghetti through paint and over the fish to 'catch' them in the net you've painted.

Peter couldn't catch any fish, but Jesus showed him where to catch hundreds. Peter was scared out of his socks, as he'd never seen anything like that before.

What do you find most amazing about Jesus?

Storms in bottles

Make a storm in a bottle.

Tell someone else the story of when Jesus told the storm to be still.

What storms are raging in your life at the moment? Try calling to Jesus, like the disciples did.

Family scrapbooking

Make a beautiful scrapbook page about the people who care for you.

When a widow's son died, Jesus brought him back to life. He cared deeply about people looking after each other.

Say a quiet 'thank you' for the people who look after you.

Party cocktails

Make a fruity cocktail, fit for a party.

Jesus healed people so that they could rejoin society. They must have had great parties to celebrate being back together with their families and friends.

Is there anyone you know who feels 'outside the party'? Could you invite them in?

House model

Make a house, with a man being let down on a mat.

Jesus healed the man from what stopped him walking and from what stopped him living life to the full on the inside.

He said, 'I have come in order that you might have life—life in all its fullness' (John 10:10, GNB)

Pustulous boils

Make a horrible wound for your arm or hand.

Jesus made people better from things much worse than this, so that they could be who they were meant to be.

What sort of person do you think you are meant to be?

Prayer stations

1) Jesus gently asks us about our deepest needs. He asked a blind man, 'What do you really want me to do for you?'
The blind man said he wanted to see, and Jesus made him see again.
Write on a speech bubble what you would really like Jesus to do for you and add it to this picture.

2) Write or draw a prayer response.

3) Add a brick on to the model and think about the way that it can grow and grow if everybody just adds one piece at a time.

How can we work miracles together to make great things grow in the world?

String telephones

Make a non-mobile phone.

What makes it easier or harder to hear the other person?

Prayer cube

Make a cube to remind you of six things to pray for: people, places, situations, friends, family...

Change the world, one prayer at a time!

When in the day could you pray with your cube?

Prayer treasure hunt

Search for the hidden letters on this treasure hunt.

Jesus told his friends that, if they looked, they would find.

Early in the morning clockwork

Make time for God.

What beautiful sculpture can you make with these materials?

Are you a morning person or a night-time person? At which time of the day do you feel closest to Jesus?

Prayer cupboards

Make a safe place to pray in.

Jesus reminded his friends not to show off by praying in front of other people to impress them, but to go into a secret place and talk to God in private.

Teaspoons

Write 't', 's' and 'p' on each of your three teaspoons.

This is a reminder of three sorts of prayers to say: Thank you, Sorry and Please.

Do you think there's anything you can't say to Jesus?

Prayer ice game

Send a coloured ice cube down the slope and over the prayer pictures.

There is so much in our world that needs transforming through our prayers!

What do you think is the best way to learn how to pray?

Doodle prayers

Bless each other with a doodle drawing!

Some people love to pray using colours and shapes rather than words.

What sort of prayers do you prefer?

Hat for a Pharisee

Make a hat for a proud, important man.

Jesus told a story about two men who prayed in different ways.

One probably wore a better hat than the other, but God was more interested in their hearts.

Bubble snakes

Make a bubble snake by blowing bubbles through a sock.

Jesus said that it would be daft if a child asked for a fish and their dad gave them a snake. Of course a dad wouldn't do that!

In the same way, God loves to give us good things, not bad things.

Prayer station

Write or draw your prayer in the sand.

Story egg box

What can you put in each eggbox hole to show the different parts of the Easter story?

Which part of it puzzles you most?

Dramatic cross

Help to make the scene dramatic.

Some very dramatic things happened while Jesus was on the cross.

Our world is in a mess. What was God's way of making it right again?

Phone photos of crosses

How many crosses can you photograph?

Jesus couldn't bring new life to us without letting go of life, dying and being buried. It was the only way.

Which cross holds most meaning for you? Why do you think the cross is such an important symbol for Christians?

Adventure challenge

Create a journey that takes people from darkness to light. Go as big as you want!

How dark did it feel for Jesus' friends on Good Friday and Saturday? But how bright it suddenly became on Sunday!

Does life feel dark or light for you at the moment? This story gives us hope, however bad things seem.

Exploding tomb sculpture

What if there was more power in Jesus' resurrection than in the explosions at the heart of the sun... or the Big Bang?

What difference does Jesus' resurrection make?

Cross section

Cross sections show you what's under the surface of something.

The cross is a mystery even to the wisest Christian.

What's under the surface of Jesus' cross? Would you add more layers of meaning?

Clean up pennies

On the cross, Jesus was making the whole world new again.

Jesus' death on the cross performed another 'miracle' to start to clean up the bad things across the whole world.

Marshmallow crosses

Make a cross and cover it in chocolate.

Is there more to Easter than chocolate?

Prayer station

Here's an icon (a picture to help you pray) of Jesus rising from the dead. Have a good look.

Write on an arrow a prayer about death. Write on another arrow a prayer about life. Stick them next to the parts of the picture that mean the most to you.

String eggs

Make a string egg to remind you of the wrapped-up body and the new life that came at Easter.

Shadow puppets

Make silhouette puppets and use them to tell the Easter story.

Which bits of the story will you choose to tell?

Index of activities